A DAY THAT CHANGED THE WORLD

GORDON BRIDGER

InterVarsity Press
Downers Grove
Illinois 60515

InterVarsity Press is the book
publishing division of Inter-Varsity
Christian Fellowship, a student
movement active on campus
at hundreds of universities, colleges and
schools of nursing. For information
about local and regional activities, write
IVCF, 233 Langdon, Madison, WI 53703.

ISBN 0-87784-483-6
Library of Congress Catalog
Card Number: 75-7246

Printed in the United States of America

Acknowledgments

There have been countless other books that have sought to explain the meaning of Jesus' death. From some of these I have gained a better understanding of the source book of the Christian faith, the Bible; and I hereby acknowledge my debt to them. No doubt my own simple attempt to write about this enormously important subject owes much to them.

I am glad to acknowledge, also, the great help I have received from the Publications Committee of the Inter-Varsity Press and their 'readers', especially in the early stages from Mrs Clare Wenham, née Richards. They can't, of course, be held responsible for the limitations that remain!

I am also grateful to Miss Ann Dakers for typing and re-typing manuscripts for me on many occasions, and to Mr Robert Manzie for help in a small item of research.

The congregation of St Thomas's Church, Corstorphine, Edinburgh, have heard all the material in this book, and much else besides, during the past five years, and are a constant source of encouragement.

Finally, I am especially grateful to my wife, Elizabeth, for her help, especially in the careful reading and checking of the final manuscript.

G. F. B.

To my wife, Elizabeth

Contents

A day that changed the world

1

It was a day they never forgot. They were both members of the Cabinet, and they had questioned the verdict of their colleagues. Now they were sure it was a mistake. This man who had been hanged on a gibbet was surely innocent. His death was little short of judicial murder. And they had watched him die.

There was little they could do now. As a gesture they asked the colonial governor whether they might be allowed to take away the man's body and give it a decent burial. This they were permitted to do.

So on that same day they removed the body from the place of execution, placed it in a garden tomb which one of them owned, and sealed the tomb with a large stone. Then they walked slowly away.

That was Friday evening. By Sunday morning something mysterious had happened. The stone had been rolled away. The tomb was empty. And a new religion was born. For the dead man was Jesus of Nazareth, and that gibbet or cross on which he died became the symbol of Christianity.

What really happened that Friday afternoon? And why should one man's *death* be so important anyway? In writing a man's biography his death is usually considered to be one of the least significant things about his story. And even where the death of a man has more importance than usual, it rarely takes up much space in the book. Take, for example, the story of Dr Martin Luther King. His death certainly shook the world, yet in one biography of him that I have read only thirty-five pages out of 362 dealt with the last days of his life.

In the biographies of Jesus which we call 'the Gospels', however, it has been estimated that almost one half of the Gospels of Matthew and Mark, one quarter of the Gospel of Luke, and one third of the Gospel of John record the last week and final hours of Jesus' life. So it seems clear that the early followers of Jesus regarded his death as of the utmost significance.

Yet there is no doubt that most people regard crucifixion with the greatest repugnance. Shame and disgrace were attached to it. It was usually reserved for only the lowest form of criminal, and certainly no citizen of Rome could be punished in this way. Indeed, the scorn of the pagans in Rome is shown only too clearly in a drawing that was discovered in the Palatine in Rome some years ago. The rough picture depicts a donkey on a gibbet and a slave kneeling before it. Underneath is the caption, 'Alexamenos worships his God.' Nothing in their view could be more despicable than worshipping a man who had been crucified.

The Jew likewise felt the shame of crucifixion. 'A hanged man is accursed by God,' said the law.[1] Yet Paul, the Jew, once he had become a Christian, could write to his friends in Corinth and say that 'of *the greatest importance*' is the fact that 'Christ died for our sins, as written in the Scriptures.' Elsewhere he could write, 'I will boast only of the cross of our Lord Jesus Christ.'

It is certainly a puzzle that anyone could speak of a Roman cross in such terms. For of all the possible ways to die it is difficult to think of any less glorious than crucifixion.

Modern man may be familiar with gas chambers, concentration camps, brain-washing, torture and similar atroci-

---

[1] Old Testament quotations are from the Revised Standard Version and New Testament quotations are from *Good News for Modern Man*. The main references are given in the 'Further reading' sections at the end of each chapter.

ties. But the ancient horror of crucifixion is generally obscured by an aura of sentimentality born out of a Christian culture and often associated with stained-glass windows and other forms of religious art. Indeed, 'the cross we bear' is far more likely to be a metaphor for severe toothache or a difficult relative than for anything bordering on real brutality. Yet the fact is that crucifixion as a means of capital punishment was every bit as agonizing and brutal as anything mankind has so far devised.

The reticence of the New Testament writers may hide this fact from us. The author of John's Gospel, for example, described the actual crucifixion of Jesus in these simple, unemotional words: 'Jesus went out . . . carrying his own cross, and came to "The Place of the Skull," as it is called. (In Hebrew it is called "Golgotha.") There they nailed him to the cross; they also nailed two other men to crosses, one on each side, with Jesus between them.'

Perhaps it was unnecessary to say more because the first-century man in the street knew only too well the horrors of death by crucifixion. But since we tend to sentimentalize the cross in the twentieth century, it would not be out of place to remind ourselves about some of the hard facts of crucifixion.

The facts about crucifixion

Imagine the prisoner staggering to the place of crucifixion, dragging himself along under the weight of the cross-beam, while the crowd around him mocked and jeered as he poured with sweat under the scorching midday sun.

Jesus would certainly have been weak from the interrogation he had had during the night, and from the lashes he had received by order of the governor. Sometimes a man died or went mad following this scourging. Small pieces of bone were inserted into the leather strips of the whip in order to bite more deeply into the flesh of the victim. By the time Jesus was ordered to carry the cross-beam to 'The Place of the Skull' outside the city walls, he was already too weak to carry it all the way. A man was press-ganged to do it for him.

When the prisoner arrived at the place of execution, the soldiers would strip him, leaving only a loin-cloth on him. They would lay the back of his neck against the cross-beam and, stretching out his arms, would hammer the nails through his wrist to the wood. Then the soldiers would take hold of the cross-beam and lift it up until the prisoner's feet were off the ground. Fixing the cross-beam to the upright, they would finally hammer a huge nail through the prisoner's feet, and leave him to suffer slow death under the hot Eastern sun. In this way Jesus was crucified.

When we consider the brutality and shame of crucifixion, it is hard to see why Joseph, a member of the Jewish Council or Sanhedrin, and Nicodemus, a learned rabbi, should risk their reputation by moving Jesus' body from the cross and by giving him a decent burial. It is even harder to understand why the early Christians regarded the cross of Jesus as both important and glorious. Somehow their natural inclinations to despise and repudiate a man dishonoured by such a death were completely overcome. Presumably they saw a significance in his death that overcame their natural reactions. What this significance is forms an important part of this book.

Ring of truth

Before we come to consider the meaning of Jesus' death, however, I must declare certain assumptions I am making in this book.

First, I am assuming that the reader accepts that Jesus really existed. We have evidence for this, of course, not only in the New Testament records, but also from pagan and Jewish sources written within 100 years of his death. It is possible to read about this evidence elsewhere.[1]

Secondly, I am assuming the substantial accuracy of the

[1] See 'Further reading' at the end of this chapter, page 14.

New Testament records of the birth, life and death of Jesus, which we call 'the Gospels', and the integrity of the New Testament writers who tell the story and interpret the events. Some years ago Sir Frederick Kenyon of the British Museum wrote a book on the Bible and archaeology, in which he said, 'Both the authenticity and the general integrity of the books of the New Testament may be regarded as finally established.' Here again the evidence for this claim lies outside the scope of this book, but may easily be found elsewhere.[1]

Above all, I am inviting the reader who may doubt the facts to examine the records themselves and to make up his own mind about their truth. In J. B. Phillips' book, *The Ring of Truth*, he expresses his view as a translator of the New Testament: 'In the whole task of translating the New Testament . . . it was the sustained down-to-earth faith of the New Testament writers which conveyed to me that inexpressible sense of the genuine and the authentic . . . It is my serious conclusion that we have here in the New Testament, words which bear the hallmark of reality and the ring of truth.'

Now clearly we have to make up our own minds as to this 'ring of truth'. But the outline of our story is straightforward enough. According to the New Testament, Jesus was born in Bethlehem in Judea in the days of Caesar Augustus. For a time he and his family were refugees in Egypt. But Jesus spent most of his early years, until he was thirty, working as a carpenter in the town of Nazareth. Then for three years he was an itinerant preacher, until he was arrested and sentenced to death by crucifixion. This was about AD 33, when Tiberius was emperor at Rome and Pontius Pilate governor of Judea. Jesus' disciples claimed that he came alive again after his death.

Our aim in this book is to consider the significance and importance of the death of Jesus of Nazareth. But first we must go back to the question we raised earlier in this chapter. Why did the early Christians attach such honour to a

[1] See 'Further reading' at the end of this chapter, page 14.

death normally associated with shame and disgrace?

One reason lies in the personality and character of Jesus himself.

Further reading

Jewish view of crucifixion: Deuteronomy 21: 23.

Christian view of crucifixion: 1 Corinthians 15: 3–8; Galatians 6: 14.

Description of Jesus' crucifixion: John 19: 17–30.

The evidence for Jesus' life is summarized in Michael Green, *Runaway World* (IVP, 1968), pages 9–38. For more detail see J. N. D. Anderson, *Christianity: the Witness of History* (Tyndale Press, 1969).

The reliability of the biblical record: see F. F. Bruce, *The New Testament Documents* (IVP, fifth edition, 1960); R. K. Harrison, *Archaeology of the New Testament* (Teach Yourself Books, EUP, 1964); F. G. Kenyon, *The Bible and Archaeology* (1940), pages 288 ff.

J. B. Phillips' *The Ring of Truth* is published by Hodder and Stoughton (1967). The quotation in this chapter is from pages 95, 96.

Who is Jesus?

'Jesus Christ Superstar
Do you think you're what they say you are?'

These words are from one of several musicals in the early
70s which caused many young people in America and in
Britain to think again about Jesus Christ.

A national newspaper, for example, carried as one of its
main features for a week a description of *Jesus Christ Superstar*. Describing this as 'the greatest story ever told' the lead-
in comment continued: 'A modern masterpiece – that is the
overwhelming verdict of all who have seen the musical, *Jesus
Christ Superstar*, in Broadway. To a background of pop
music, the last seven days in the life of Christ are portrayed
in a way that has astounded America and is now setting
Britain talking. *It is a must for all who seek to comprehend the
new significance of Jesus Christ – the man, the Messiah, the
revolutionary – to Britain's young people today.*'

Following the *Superstar* sensation, another musical,
Godspell, its script based clearly on the story in Matthew's
Gospel, took London by storm. Meanwhile, in a more
serious vein, there came news of the Jesus Revolution in
America. Hundreds of drop-outs and hippies spoke of their
lives being changed by Jesus. Posters began to appear in
America and Britain along the following lines:

WANTED:

JESUS CHRIST

Notorious Leader of an underground liberation movement.
Wanted on the following charges:
Practising medicine, wine-making and food distribution without a licence.
Interfering with businessmen in the Temple.
Associating with known criminals, radicals, subversives, prostitutes, and street people.
Claiming to have the authority to make people into God's children.

APPEARANCE:
Typical hippie type— long hair, beard, robe, sandals.
Hangs around slum areas, few rich friends, often sneaks out into the desert.
BEWARE
—this man is extremely dangerous. His insidiously inflammatory message is particularly dangerous to young people who haven't been taught to ignore him yet.
He changes men and claims to set them free.
WARNING: HE IS STILL AT LARGE

The mass media began to probe the significance of this Jesus Movement. Once more the name of Jesus was upon the lips of people – many of whom regarded themselves as outside the established churches and organized religions. But what *kind* of Jesus are people talking about?

The person portrayed in *Jesus Christ Superstar* is very far removed from the Jesus of the New Testament, though certain aspects of his character do parallel the Jesus of the Gospels. Jesus Superstar possesses courage and single-mindedness. He fights injustice, cares for the handicapped and identifies himself with the unwanted. He certainly would rather die than compromise.

So far so good. But beyond this point Superstar hopelessly fails to fit the facts of the New Testament. According to the opera, he becomes less and less sure of his calling as the years go by. His crusade of three years, he sings, feels like thirty. So he is crucified, forgotten by God, his task unfulfilled. He is, after all, no more than a disillusioned idealist. A good man, but no more than a man.

The New Testament writers, however, *were* convinced that Jesus was more than a man. They came to believe that he was truly human and truly divine. What evidence is there for such a claim?

Jesus' character

If a man claims to be perfect, it is usually regarded as the ultimate in big-headedness, or as evidence of a deranged mind. The extraordinary thing about the life of Jesus is that his claims to be perfect ring true.

When Jesus says, 'I always do the things that please the Father,' his closest friends cannot but agree with him. 'There is no sin in him,' wrote John later. When Jesus said one day to his critics, 'Which of you can prove that I am guilty of sin?' they were stunned; no-one contradicted him.

All the evidence shows that Jesus lived a perfect life. His personality, we are told, was 'full of grace and truth'.

His whole way of life was loving, humble and selfless. Even a leading humanist once said wistfully of Jesus, 'If only we could be infected by his spirit.'

Of course it is possible that the New Testament writers deliberately whitewashed Jesus' character. But it is hard to believe this on the evidence of the New Testament as a whole. The authors of the Gospels are scrupulously honest in their record of the faults of the other chief characters in the story, such as Peter, James and John. Furthermore, it is hard to believe that any man could have produced a fictional character like Jesus – a man so free of insipid goody-goodness, yet with the perfect purity of the New Testament Jesus.

It is even harder to imagine that such a writer would have invented Jesus' other claims about himself. For at first sight these appear to point to delusions rather than to divinity. Yet part of Jesus' teaching is certainly taken up with his own claims to be unique and divine.

Jesus' claims

It is surprising how often Jesus' claims about himself are overlooked today.

'Jesus Christ Superstar
Do you think you're what they say you are?'

If 'they' means the church with its view that Jesus is divine, then there is no doubt that, according to the New Testament record, Jesus thought this about himself. Although he always accepted that he was born normally, Jesus referred to his origins in this way: 'I came from God'; 'I . . . came down from heaven.' When he spoke about his own teaching, he said, 'The message you have heard is not mine, but comes from the Father, who sent me,' and 'Heaven and earth will pass away; my words will never pass away.'

Furthermore, when he spoke of his relationship with his heavenly Father, he was able to say, 'The Father and I are one.' He often claimed to be equal with God: 'Whoever has seen me has seen the Father.' 'Whoever believes in me, believes not only in me but also in him who sent me.' 'Whoever receives me, receives him who sent me.' 'Whoever does not honour the Son does not honour the Father who sent him.'

Sometimes he used God's name as his own. 'Before Abraham was born, "I Am",' he said to his critics on one occasion. The words 'I Am' represented a title for God that the Jew, out of reverence, would never take upon his lips. Jesus, however, claimed the right to use these words about himself.

Sometimes in his preaching Jesus assumed the right to forgive sins, to give men eternal life and to settle men's destiny. No wonder the critics raised the question, 'But who can do this but God?' It was a proper question to ask. Could a mere man speak in this way about himself?

He might if he were deluded. But there is no sign of delusion or megalomania in the balanced life and ministry of Jesus. He might if he were divine. That is what the early Christians came to believe was the only answer that fitted the facts.

John wrote of Jesus as the 'Word'. 'Before the world was created, the Word already existed; he was with God, and he was the same as God.' 'The Word became a human being and lived among us.' 'The full content of the divine nature lives in Christ,' wrote Paul. Now this view of Jesus is further corroborated if we consider his supernatural deeds.

Jesus' 'miracles'

The early Christian preachers were able to speak without fear of contradiction about the 'signs' and 'miracles' that Jesus did. Furthermore, there is as good documentary evidence in the New Testament for the miracles of Jesus as for any other aspect of his life and teaching.

It is interesting, too, that the early Jewish critics of Christianity do not deny that Jesus did 'miracles', but only deny the divine source of them. Even the pagan philosopher Celsus, who wrote an influential attack on the Christian faith in the second century, does not attempt to deny that Jesus had miraculous powers. He attributed them to sorcery.

Now it would have been natural for stories of Jesus to have been exaggerated over the years. Some of the so-called 'Apocryphal Gospels' – stories of Jesus written in the second and third centuries – show every sign of this. What is remarkable and different about the miracles of the New Testament, however, is the absence of exaggeration and gimmickry. Clearly they are used by Jesus as 'visual aids' for his teaching. They are 'signs' as well as 'wonders'.

There was one sign that Jesus said was more important than any other. No man has ever been able to assert that he would die and rise again from the dead and then keep his word – except Jesus of Nazareth. At least, that is the claim that is made in the New Testament.

'I am willing to give up my life, in order that I may receive it back again,' said Jesus. On another occasion he said, 'The Son of Man (a title he used for himself) must suffer much . . . He will be put to death, and after three days he will be raised to life.'

If Jesus was able to fulfil such a promise, then surely this endorses all the *claims* he made about his deity. What then is the evidence for his resurrection?

Further reading

Jesus' character: John 8: 29, 30, 46; 2 Corinthians 5: 21; 1 Peter 2: 22; 1 John 3: 5.
Jesus' claims: Matthew 24: 35; Mark 2: 1–12; John 3: 13; 5: 23; 8: 42, 58; 10: 30; 12: 44–50; 13: 20; 14: 9, 24.
Jesus predicts his death: Mark 8: 31; John 10: 17.
See also Gordon Bridger, *The Man from Outside* (IVP, 1969); John R. W. Stott, *Basic Christianity* (IVP, second edition, 1971).

Did Jesus rise from the dead?

Down the years, many have attacked the Christian claim that Jesus rose from the dead. Some of Jesus' contemporaries also were sceptical of this claim. When Thomas, one of Jesus' disciples, heard that other disciples had seen Jesus alive, at first he could not believe it and said, 'If I do not see the scars of the nails in his hands, and put my finger where the nails were, and my hand in his side, I will *not* believe.'

Another man who was at first sceptical of the preaching of the early Christians concerning Jesus and the resurrection was the brilliant and zealous young Jewish rabbi, Saul of Tarsus, who later was called Paul. Paul was one of the bright young intellectuals who sat at the feet of the famous teacher, Gamaliel, in the 'University' of Jerusalem. His trained mind was eager to dispose of the arguments of the Christians. His religious fanaticism caused him to persecute every Christian he could find. He could not and would not believe that Jesus had risen from the dead. Then, suddenly and incredibly, he began to preach that Jesus *had* risen – that Jesus had appeared to him alive!

It is difficult to imagine why a man like Paul should become a Christian, unless he was absolutely convinced that the Christian claims were true. It is not only that he was an intellectual who would quickly see through weak arguments or faulty evidence. He was also a promising young rabbi, with a rosy future before him academically and socially.

He had nothing to gain, humanly speaking, from becoming a Christian. He would be exchanging a life of honour and prestige, to throw in his lot with, for the most part, a crowd of fishermen and slaves. He knew that he would inevitably be meeting scorn, ostracism, persecution and almost certainly a violent death – and he a Roman citizen too! What changed his mind?

Now the exciting thing is that we have a good source for the answer to that question. We have a letter written by Paul not more than twenty-seven years after the resurrection and probably earlier. In it he sets out some of the reasons for his change of heart and mind.

The fact of the empty tomb

No-one denies that the tomb was empty. Paul refers to it briefly when he says, 'I passed on to you what I received, which is of the greatest importance: that Christ died for our sins, as written in the Scriptures; *that he was buried* and raised to life on the third day.' There was no point in adding 'he was buried' unless he wanted to draw attention to the empty tomb.

Of course there have been attempts to substitute other explanations for the empty tomb. But no-one can reasonably deny, on the evidence, that it was empty.

Some have suggested that *the disciples stole the body*, and pretended that Jesus had risen from the dead. But this is hardly likely, not only because soldiers had been placed there to prevent this very thing, but also because the disciples had no real motive to do this. Even if we suppose they did do it, it is still hard to believe that they could have endured persecution and given their lives for something they knew to be false. And do we really believe that all Jesus' friends would have kept the secret of where the body was taken?

Others have agreed that *the enemies of Jesus could have removed the body*. But when within a few weeks of the crucifixion Peter was telling the crowds that 'God has raised Jesus from the dead, and *we are all witnesses to this fact*', why did not someone step forward and say, 'Don't be stupid; I can show you the body'? If either the Roman or Jewish enemies of Jesus had removed the body, they had only to produce it or indicate its whereabouts to crush the faith of the disciples overnight. There is no doubt that many wanted to stamp out this Christian movement, but the fact is that no such evidence against the Christian case could be produced.

In recent years, an old theory that *Jesus never really died, but only swooned* – perhaps under influence of a drug – has been advanced. Again, this ignores all the New Testament evidence, especially the detailed evidence about the grave-clothes that we read about in John's Gospel. John makes clear that the grave-clothes were still lying in the tomb undisturbed and 'collapsed'. That is, they had not been removed and thrown in a heap in a corner. But they still looked as if they were round the body. They were 'collapsed' presumably because of the weight of the spices that would have been placed between the folds. So John gives the impression that not a fold of the 'linen cloths' was out of place, and that the turban was 'rolled up by itself' – that is, lying just where the head had been. When John saw *this*, he believed.

Quite apart from this, it is hard to believe that a man could survive a Roman scourging and the horrors of cruci-fixion, and still manage to throw off his tightly bound grave-clothes, roll away the heavy stone boulder and, in spite of all the physical suffering he had endured, manage to convince his followers that he was conquering death and the grave. Some-times modern readers are expected to swallow rather a lot!

The fact of Jesus' appearances

Paul strengthens his case still further by recording a num-ber of occasions when Jesus appeared alive, after his cruci-fixion, to his disciples. This is what he says: 'He appeared to Peter, and then to all twelve apostles. Then he appeared to more than five hundred of his followers at once, most of whom are still alive, although some have died. Then he appeared to James, and then to all the apostles.'

If we add to this list of 'appearances' the evidence of the Gospels, there are at least eleven separate occasions when Jesus was seen and recognized by disciples after his crucifixion. Certainly Jesus was not always recognized at first sight. For one thing the disciples were obviously not expecting to see him, even though he had told them before his crucifixion that he would rise again from the dead. When they did recognize him, however, they saw that his body bore the marks of his recent suffering – there were marks in his hands and side. They also record that, although he was recognizable, he was able to appear and disappear suddenly, even through closed doors. On one occasion Jesus told the disciples clearly that he was not a 'ghost' or 'spirit' and he ate some fish in front of them to prove it!

Now no doubt we find this difficult to explain. But the fact that the disciples clearly did not expect to see Jesus when he appeared to them, and that he appeared to as many as 500 men on one occasion, rules out the theory that the disciples were suffering from hallucinations. The sure mark of hallucinations is that they come to *individuals* who are *expecting* to see what they imagine they see. Furthermore, if the disciples were having hallucinations they would surely have seen Jesus as he was when they had last seen him alive. In fact they saw nail-prints and the mark of the sword thrust in his side.

Now Paul is no fool. As he soberly states his case, he invites his readers to check his story: some of the 500 men who saw the risen Jesus are still alive to tell the tale, he says. Indeed, he is so convinced that the evidence is true that he makes the death and resurrection of Jesus the foundation truths of his whole life and ministry: 'If Christ has not been raised from death, then we have nothing to preach, and you have nothing to believe. More than that, we are shown to be lying against God.'

The fact of a changed life

Paul's case for the resurrection of Jesus did not depend only on the evidence of the empty tomb and the eye-witness account of Jesus' appearances to the disciples. Paul could also say, 'Last of all he appeared also to me.'

For Paul's encounter with the risen Jesus on the Damascus road not only convinced him but changed him.

Let him tell the story in his own words: 'Last of all he appeared also me. . . . I do not even deserve to be called an apostle, because I persecuted God's church. But by God's grace I am what I am, and the grace that he gave me was not without effect. On the contrary, I have worked harder than all the other apostles, although it was not really my own doing, but God's grace working with me. So then, whether it came from me or from them, this is what we all preach, this is what you believe.'

Paul the persecutor of Christians had become Paul the Christian preacher!

It was not only Paul, of course, whose life had been changed by the resurrection of Jesus. At least I can find no other reason that explains the change in the behaviour of the other disciples. After Jesus' crucifixion they were fearful and disillusioned, and hiding behind closed doors. A few weeks later they were bold and joyful, and preaching that Jesus had risen from the dead! Something significant must be behind that change.

This same letter to the Christians at Corinth has further examples of people's behaviour being completely changed. Corinth was a seaport, notorious for its immorality. 'To Corinthianize' was a Greek idiom which roughly meant 'to go to hell'. No doubt the sexual permissiveness was further stimulated by Corinth's patronage of the organized worship of the 'goddess of love'. Yet from that city, men and women who were up to the neck in vice were changed into followers of Christ. Paul's own words make that undeniable: 'Do not fool yourselves: people who are immoral, or worship idols, or are adulterers, or homosexual perverts, or who rob, or are greedy, or are drunkards, or who slander others, or are lawbreakers – none of these will receive God's Kingdom. *Some of you were like that.* But you have been cleansed from sin; you have been dedicated to God; you have been put right with God through the name of the Lord Jesus Christ, and by the Spirit of our God.' Could lives have been changed in that way by a message based on a lie?

Clearly the case of Jesus' resurrection was a strong one in those early days. Apart from this passage in Paul's letter to Corinth, the rest of the New Testament letters can assume the fact of the resurrection without any need, apparently, to marshal the evidence or repeat the arguments. The empty tomb, the appearance of Jesus, and the changed lives of the disciples could not easily be rejected.

There is one further fact that we should add for completeness.

The fact of the Christian church

At the time of Jesus' death his disillusioned followers did not look likely leaders of a new religious movement that would spread throughout the civilized world. Yet the continued existence and growth of the Christian church down the years, the degree to which it has influenced our civilization for good, and the continued testimony of Christians to a Jesus who is alive are facts that also demand an explanation.

Take, for example, the way in which Christians have faced up to suffering and death. Aristotle, the great philosopher, said, 'Death is a dreadful thing; it is the end.' Yet the apostle Paul could say, because of Jesus' resurrection, 'What is life? To me, it is Christ! Death, then, will bring something better.' None of the early Christians seemed afraid to die.

About 100 years later an old man called Polycarp stood before a Roman governor in Smyrna, a town in what is now Turkey. The issue was clear. If he did not curse Christ, he would either be thrown to the lions or burned at the stake. But Polycarp not only believed that Jesus had conquered death; he knew him as a living friend. 'For eighty-six years I have been his servant, and he has done me no wrong. How can I blaspheme my King who saved me?' He went to his death rejoicing.

Today it is no different. In the appalling massacres in Burundi in 1972 many Christians were killed and others cruelly beaten. One African schoolmaster who had been severely beaten said, 'Before this happened my faith in Jesus was more like an intellectual acceptance of the truth of the gospel. But now I know that Jesus is real. When I was in that prison Jesus came and his presence and love were so real and wonderful to me, I felt no pain from the blows. I thought I was already in heaven. I live for the day when I shall feel Jesus as close to me again as he was in that prison.'

Again, countless ordinary Christians, in far less dramatic circumstances and in every walk of life, are equally convinced that Jesus is alive. A woman wrote in a letter to me: 'I was brought up to go to church – but it was not until I lost my only son in a car crash that I realized that what I had was only the veneer of Christianity. In my despair, misery and self-pity, I begged Jesus for strength. . . . He has given me this and more, the gift of himself in my heart.'

For these Christians it is the conviction that Jesus is alive and with them that enables them to face suffering and death with calm and confidence. Were they all deluded?

The evidence of Jesus' resurrection cannot be dismissed lightly. If it is true that Jesus rose from the dead, and there is strong evidence to support this, then Jesus' other claims about himself are endorsed. For, in the apostle Paul's words, 'He was shown with great power to be the Son of God, by being raised from death.' If Jesus is God become man, as the New Testament affirms, then it is not surprising but utterly fitting that death could not destroy him.

The question we now have to ask is why the God-Man,

Jesus, needed to die at all. Why was it necessary anyway?
And what were the reasons that led up to his death?

Further reading

Thomas's doubts: John 20: 24–29.
The empty tomb: John 20: 1–10.
Eye-witnesses: Acts 2: 32; 3: 15.
Jesus' appearances: 1 Corinthians 15: 3–7; to Paul, 15: 8–11.
The foundation truth of Christianity: 1 Corinthians 15: 14, 15.
Changed lives: 1 Corinthians 6: 9–11.
Christian attitude to death: 1 Corinthians 15: 51–56; Philippians 1: 21.

For more detail on Jesus' resurrection, see J. N. D. Anderson, *The Evidence for the Resurrection* (IVP, 1950); Michael Green, *Man Alive!* (IVP, 1967); Frank Morison, *Who Moved the Stone?* (Faber and Faber, 1944).

What led up to Jesus' death?

'A bloody, dusty, sweaty, and sordid business': this is how Dorothy Sayers describes the death of Jesus. She wrote, 'His executioners made vulgar jokes about him, called him petty names, taunted him, smacked him in the face, flogged him with a cat and hanged him on a common gibbet.' Yet in spite of the brutality and the shame of crucifixion, the early Christians, as we have seen, believed that Jesus' death had great 'significance' and 'honour'.

So far we have argued that, according to all the evidence of the New Testament documents, this same Jesus claimed to be God during his lifetime, and that his resurrection from the dead convincingly endorses that claim. Why, then, did this man Jesus, who claimed to be God, have to die? How had God come to be sentenced to death?

On a superficial level certain straightforward reasons for the crucifixion of Jesus emerge.

Professional jealousy

It is not unusual for men to envy people who are more successful than they are. And when Jesus had been preaching, people were amazed at the way he taught. He was not like the teachers of the law; instead he taught with authority. Wherever he taught, the people compared the authority and clarity of his speaking with the hesitancies and uncertainties of the scribes, the professional theologians of their day. They also contrasted his simple life and understanding manner with the proud and extravagant life-style of the Pharisees.

So some of the religious leaders did all they could to discredit him in the eyes of the people. They saw him as largely self-taught. He had not been to the right theological colleges. Nor had he the right accent. After Jesus' first sermon in the synagogue at Nazareth, they started murmuring, 'Where did he get such wisdom ? . . . Isn't he the carpenter's son ? Isn't Mary his mother ?'

On one occasion Jesus suggested that God cared as much for the non-Jews as for the Jews themselves, and that these Gentiles sometimes showed more faith and compassion than God's own people. 'There were many widows in Israel during the time of Elijah,' he had reminded them. 'Yet Elijah was not sent to a single one of them, but only to a widow of Zaraphath, in the territory of Sidon.' At this they tried to kill Jesus.

Some of them were no less annoyed when Jesus told the story of the man who showed concern for the victim of a mugging incident on the Jericho road. For it was a Samaritan and not a Jew who showed love for his neighbour that day. Once they queried the legitimacy of his birth. '*We* were not born of fornication,' they sneered.

At other times they tried to trip him up with trick questions. Some Pharisees came to him and tried to trap him by asking, 'Does our law allow a man to divorce his wife for any and every reason . . . ?'

Opposition from the top

There is no doubt that this was what put teeth into their hostility. For Annas and Caiaphas seemed to be the chief instigators of the more hostile pressures against Jesus.

Annas was probably the power behind the throne.

A notorious and much-hated figure in Jerusalem, he had been high priest from AD 6 to AD 15. At one time the office of high priest had been held for life, but under the Romans high priests 'came and went like flies in a sore', according to Tiberius. The office was often open to the highest bidder, and the man most willing to collaborate with the Roman governor.

Four of Annas' sons had become, or were to become, high priests. Caiaphas, the high priest who tried Jesus, was Annas' son-in-law. And as Annas and his family almost certainly ran the notorious 'bazaars' in the Temple, exploiting the luckless pilgrims, it is not surprising that they became exceedingly wealthy. So when Jesus attacked the exploitation of pilgrims in the Temple precincts, at the start and the end of his ministry, it may well be that he became a marked man in the eyes of Annas and Co. When religion touches a man's pocket, it hurts.

No doubt some Jewish leaders had other motives. For example, we read: 'So the Pharisees and the chief priests met with the Council and said: "What shall we do? All the mighty works this man is doing! If we let him go on in this way everyone will believe in him, and the Roman authorities will take action and destroy the Temple and our whole nation!"'

Whatever the motives were, it is certainly true that as Jesus became more popular with the man in the street, the hostility on the part of some of the religious leaders grew. They began to plot subtle ways to do away with him. We read: 'The chief priests and the teachers of the Law were trying to find a way of killing Jesus; for they were afraid of the people'; 'The chief priests and the Jewish elders met together in the palace of Caiaphas, the high priest, and made plans to arrest Jesus secretly and put him to death.'

In the event, Judas Iscariot, one of Jesus' band of disciples, whose heart was not with Jesus in his ministry, gave them the chance they wanted. For love of money, and possibly for other reasons as well, Judas offered to lead Jesus' enemies to a quiet place away from the crowds, where they could arrest him without trouble. And this they did.

The treachery of Judas was no less than the hostility of the Jewish leaders. Even so, the New Testament writers recognize that none of those who were responsible for the crucifixion of Jesus understood the full significance of what they were doing. That night, however, Jesus was brought before the religious leaders and tried by the Sanhedrin.

Injustice in the courts

The Sanhedrin had a reputation for justice. It prided itself on the way it acted as 'counsel for the defence' for a man on trial. But in the case of Jesus' trial, this certainly did not happen.

'Sentence of death shall be carried out on the testimony of two or three witnesses; no one shall be put to death on the testimony of a single witness.' This is what the Jewish law laid down. But we are told by Mark that 'many witnesses told lies against Jesus, but their stories did not agree'.

Again, according to Jewish law, the Sanhedrin could meet officially only in the Hall of Hewn Stone in the precincts of the Temple. No capital trial could be held at night, nor could a verdict of guilty be proclaimed till the following day. Jesus, however, was arrested at night, and taken first to Annas and then to the house of Caiaphas for a preliminary examination. He was asked questions to incriminate himself – contrary to Jewish law – and he was subjected to physical violence. The final verdict was given against Jesus the same evening as the trial.

The only agreed case against Jesus was that he had said something about destroying the Temple in three days, and that he was guilty of blasphemy. But the Sanhedrin knew perfectly well that these charges would not be considered capital offences by the Roman authorities. So the Sanhedrin added perjury to their crimes by fabricating three other charges of a political nature. According to Luke, these accusations were that (1) Jesus was a revolutionary; (2) he was acting as an enemy to the state by inciting people not to pay their taxes; and (3) he claimed to be king.

Jesus was an embarrassment to the top men of his day. His words and life exposed their hypocrisy and injustice and greed. He must be made to suffer. For men will go to any lengths to cover up wrongdoing. Men love darkness rather than light.

Weakness of the Roman governor

The Jews were aided in their terrible task by the weakness of the Roman authorities. Rome too prided herself on her standards of justice, and in many instances she was right to do so.

Pilate, the governor at the time, must have been an able administrator to have been offered such a difficult job in the Civil Service of Rome. But history tells us that he had little sympathy with or understanding of the Jews in Palestine, and often treated them with great cruelty and brutality. As a result, the Jewish leaders had already threatened to report him to the emperor, Tiberius, for his mishandling of earlier affairs.

This may have been at the back of his mind when he weakly tried to avoid making any decision about Jesus, seeking to wash his hands of the whole affair. Yet, when the religious leaders said, 'If you set him free that means you are not the Emperor's friend,' it frightened Pilate sufficiently for him to hand Jesus over to be crucified.

Pilate had certainly said he could find no fault with Jesus, that he was not 'worthy of death'. But fear of losing his job, or of loss of prestige, drove him to allow a travesty of justice that has sullied his name ever since.

The jealousy and injustice of the religious leaders and the weakness of the secular authority – the governor, Pontius Pilate – are two obvious human factors that led to the crucifixion of Jesus of Nazareth. Yet it is clear that Jesus could have avoided death, as his closest friends pointed out to him. In fact, he walked into trouble.

On a number of occasions Jesus told his disciples that he *must* suffer many things, and be rejected by the elders, the chief priests and the scribes: 'I will be put to death, and on the third day I will be raised to life.' When Peter ridiculed this suggestion, Jesus rebuked him with the words of utmost severity: 'Get away from me, Satan! You are an obstacle in my way, for these thoughts of yours are men's thoughts, not God's!' For Peter it was defeatist talk to mention inevitable death. For Jesus any attempt, however well-meaning, to divert him from a path of suffering leading to death was inspired by Satan, not by God.

From early days Jesus seemed to know that his destiny was to suffer an early death, yet he could say, 'I am willing to give up my life, in order that I may receive it back again. No one takes my life away from me. I give it up of my own free will.'

So however much some men may have plotted the death of Jesus, the evidence suggests that Jesus took no avoiding action, and that he laid down his life voluntarily.

Why, then, did Jesus choose to die?

Further reading

Opposition from the Jewish leaders: Matthew 13: 53–57; 26: 3–5; Luke 4: 25–30; 22: 2; John 11: 47–53.
Jesus before the high priest: Mark 14: 53–65; 15: 1.
Jesus before Pilate: John 18: 28–19: 16.
Jesus' attitude to death: Matthew 16: 21–23; John 10: 17, 18.

Why did Jesus choose to die?

5

At first sight the death of Jesus might be supposed to be no more significant than the martyrdom of other great men who have died for a noble cause, or who have unselfishly sacrificed their lives for the sake of others.

Take, for example, the moving account of the death of a British soldier in Ernest Gordon's book, *Miracle on the River Kwai*. The scene is set in a Japanese prisoner-of-war camp. After a day's work carried out by the soldiers and supervised by Japanese guards, one of the guards who is checking the tools shouts that a shovel is missing. He insists that one of the British prisoners has stolen it to sell to the Thais. In a furious rage he demands that the guilty one steps forward to take his punishment. No one moves. The guard shrieks, 'All die! All die!' He cocks his rifle to fire. At that moment an Argyll soldier steps forward, stands stiffly to attention, and says calmly, 'I did it.' Instantly he is killed. The men pick up their comrade's body, shoulder their tools, and march back to camp. Later, when the tools are counted again at the guardhouse it is found that *no shovel is missing*. The Argyll was innocent. He voluntarily laid down his life that his comrades might live.

Just a hero?

Is Jesus' death all that different from the moving sacrificial act which I have just described? It is sometimes suggested that his death was no more than an act of heroism. Certainly we could describe the soldier's death in this way. And history has many heroic martyrs. Was Jesus, then, a heroic martyr dying for a lost cause? A Superstar who eventually died rather than compromise?

There is no doubt about Jesus' heroism. It is one thing for a man to rise to a heroic act on the spur of the moment. It is surely even more heroic to set one's face to go into trouble and certain death. And that is how the New Testament describes his attitude, as we saw in the last chapter.

One Gospel records how Jesus walked in front of his disciples, firmly set to go to Jerusalem where his enemies were waiting for him. The disciples were afraid. But not Jesus.

Just before his arrest and trial, we read that Jesus was in great agony of mind, and prayed, 'Father, if you will, take this cup away from me. Not my will, however, but your will be done.' Yet finally he did not shrink from the ordeal. His calmness and dignity before the authorities, and his courage in bearing the pain of crucifixion, are convincing enough examples of his heroism.

Yet surely this is nothing but foolhardiness unless by dying he accomplished something. And on the evidence of the New Testament his death certainly did mean much more than an act of heroism.

Just a good example?

Some have suggested that Jesus' death was a demonstration of his love for us, and an example to inspire us. Now a sacrificial death for others *can* be a great inspiration. And certainly, as Jesus once said, 'The greatest love a man can have for his friends is to give his life for them.' Indeed, in the case of

36

the Argyll, the soldier's courage in stepping forward and dying for something he had not done was one of the factors that led to a change in the morale in that prisoner-of-war camp which at that time was desperately low. Once again men began to think of other people before themselves. A new spirit of caring love began to appear. Some of the men began to be ashamed of their own selfishness and began to want to change.

Was this the supreme importance of Jesus' death – an example of selfless sacrificial love, to inspire others to live no longer for themselves, but for God and for others? As we shall see later, this is true as far as it goes. Peter writes to Christians who are discouraged by the persecution they face, and reminds them of the example of Jesus' suffering and death. 'Christ himself suffered for you and left you an example, so that you would follow in his steps.'

The death of Christ can, and does, inspire men. But man needs more than inspiration. If a man who cannot swim is drowning in the river, what is the best way to help him? By jumping in heroically, demonstrating your love for him, and no more? By showing him by example how he could use his arms and legs to swim to the nearest bank? Or by doing for him what he cannot do for himself – actually getting alongside, putting strong arms around him, and rescuing him? Obviously if a man needs rescuing he needs more than an example, or a demonstration of heroism: he needs a rescuer. As we read the New Testament we begin to see that the death of Jesus had something to do with 'rescuing' or 'saving' people, and doing for them what they could not do for themselves.

But why do people need rescuing? And how can Jesus' death 2,000 years ago have anything to do with it? We cannot answer these questions until we are clear about man's actual need and God's reaction to it. And we shall best understand that if we think first about the character of God.

Further reading

Jesus' heroism: Mark 10: 32; Luke 22: 42–44.
Jesus' example: 1 Peter 2: 21–23.

E. Gordon's *Miracle on the River Kwai* is published by Fontana Books (1965). The story referred to is from page 88.

What is God like?

6

A small inquisitive child began to ask her mother some awkward questions. 'Mummy,' she said, 'is God in this house?' 'Yes,' said her mother, 'God is everywhere.' 'Is God in this kitchen, then?' went on the child. 'Why, yes,' said her mother. 'Is he on this table?' 'Well,' said the mother, trying to remember snatches of theology from the sermons she had heard, 'Well, I think so.' 'Is he in this inkpot?' the child continued remorselessly. 'Well, yes, I suppose so,' replied her mother. The girl slammed her small hand down on top of the inkpot. 'Got him!' she shouted triumphantly.

Many of us have probably treated God like that at times. We have tried to 'bottle' him, to hold him in our grasp, to manipulate him, to bring him down to our size, our convenience. Some people, on the other hand, like to keep God at a distance by regarding him as nothing more than some vague impersonal force or power. Others think of him as some benevolent, grandfatherly figure who overlooks all our shortcomings.

It is easy enough and more comfortable for man to make God in his own image. Sometimes we make him hardly bigger than ourselves. But the God of the Bible is different. He is described as spirit, the eternal God who is 'from everlasting to everlasting', as well as in more personal terms, a loving heavenly Father. He both made and sustains the universe by the word of his power. He is sovereign and

Lord over all. He holds kings, emperors and dictators in his hands and uses them when he chooses as his instruments. He sets up one and puts down another. He rules over all.

An early Christian preacher put it like this: 'God, who made the world and everything in it, is Lord of heaven and earth, and does not live in temples made by men. Nor does he need anything that men can supply by working for him, since it is he himself who gives life and breath and everything else to all men. From the one man he created all races of men, and made them to live over the whole earth. He himself fixed beforehand the exact times and the limits of the places where they would live. He did this so that they would look for him, and perhaps find him as they felt around for him. Yet God is actually not far from any one of us; for "In him we live and move and are." '

Many of us, however, not only limit the greatness of God, but also misunderstand his character. Yet it is a proper understanding of the character of God that is vital for us if we are to understand why Jesus' death was necessary.

God's character

1. God is love. A central belief of the Christian faith is that God is love. But the love of God is different from mere human emotion. When we speak about 'falling in love' we often refer to a passing feeling for another person. A man may 'fall out of love' as quickly as he 'falls in love'. Such human emotion is sometimes here today and gone tomorrow.

But God's love is not like that. Certainly God is said to be 'full of compassion'. But his love, unlike our feelings of love, is always there. It is an everlasting love. It is part of the very nature of God, and was expressed, according to Jesus, even before the creation of the world. 'You loved me', he said in a prayer to his heavenly Father, 'before the world was made.' God's essential nature is love. He is always loving. God *is* love.

God's love is also different from human friendship in some

respects. We may truly love our friends, and say sincerely that we would do anything for them. We might be prepared to make sacrifices for them, and even in exceptional circumstances to lay down our life for them. But human friendship is rarely, if ever, free of some selfish motive. Often we cease to show friendship if we get nothing in return from our friend. And we very rarely love our enemies consistently.

God calls those who believe in him his 'friends', and loves them. Abraham was called the friend of God. Jesus told his disciples that he would call them no longer servants but friends. But God's love extends also to his enemies. As Jesus himself taught, God 'makes his sun to shine on bad and good people alike, and gives rain to those who do right and those who do wrong'.

2. God is holy. There is another aspect of God's character which we easily forget, which the Bible consistently teaches. It is that God is holy. The love which God expresses, therefore, must be consistent with his holiness. It cannot be any kind of love that someone with a sentimental view of God might imagine. It must be a holy love.

The word 'holy' implies that God is 'distinct and different' and 'separate' from all others. 'High and lifted up', as one Old Testament writer expressed it. But God's holiness is not simply a passive idea. God expresses his holiness in reacting positively against all that is unholy; in fact, all that falls short of God's own standard of perfection.

'God is light and there is no darkness at all in him,' wrote the Christian apostle John. But such a metaphor not only points out that God is 'different' from all those who 'walk in darkness'; it also shows that God, who is the light, cannot live with man who walks in darkness. The light banishes the darkness, just as God, in his holiness, had to banish disobedient man from his presence, in the story of the Garden of Eden.

For most of us it is difficult to imagine the holy love of God. We find it hard to accept that a loving God can act with such moral strictness against disobedient man. But then we have little idea of what perfect love and perfect holiness mean and do not find it easy to see how they unite in the character of God.

If, however, we look at Jesus' life and ministry, we can see how these two aspects of the divine character unite in him. There is no suspicion of Jesus being a split personality. He acted consistently in holy love towards all he met.

One example from Jesus' life must suffice. As Jesus went about 'doing good' it is obvious that he loved people and really cared for their best interests. Yet, when he met a prostitute at the well in Samaria, his love is seen in his friendliness and concern for her, and his holiness in the relentless way in which he puts his finger on the moral failure in her life, so that it might be confessed and forsaken. Jesus never treated wrongdoing and disobedience lightly. He could never overlook it or condone it, however much he loved the wrongdoer.

'I haven't got a husband,' said the woman in the course of her conversation with Jesus. 'You are right when you say you haven't got a husband,' replied Jesus. 'The man you live with now is not really your husband.' In this incident Jesus was offering the woman a new and satisfying kind of life possible to those who believed in him. But he makes it clear that a new life cannot be received unless wrongdoing is renounced.

God's holy love is like that. He loves us with infinite love. He hates wrongdoing and shows it up in its true colours, that it may be dealt with and finished with. 'Our God', said the Christian writer of the letter to the Hebrews, 'is a destroying fire.' Fire both warms and destroys. It is not only, as one Old Testament writer put it, that God is too pure to be able to look at evil; in his holy love God must banish all evildoers from his presence. Light and darkness cannot coexist.

There is one further aspect of God's character which we must consider at this point.

3. God is righteous or just. In Britain we pride ourselves on our standards of justice in the courts. Our judges have a world-wide reputation for integrity and fair play. We would be appalled if serious allegations were made about bending the laws to obstruct the course of justice. We recognize that lawlessness and chaos would undoubtedly follow if justice were allowed to go by default.

According to the Bible, God is a just judge, as well as a loving heavenly Father. His moral laws are found, for example, in the Ten Commandments and in the Sermon on the Mount. This justice is expressed in the judgments that follow the breaking of those laws. Certainly when these laws are broken or ignored, moral chaos and lawlessness follow. Would we not be appalled if God 'turned a blind eye' to the breaking of these laws, and failed to judge the wrongdoers?

The just reaction of God's holy love against all who break the law is sometimes described as 'the wrath of God'. So the apostle Paul could speak of the way in which God was judging the society of his own day by writing that 'God's wrath is revealed coming down from heaven upon all the sin and evil of men, whose evil ways prevent the truth from being known.' The final day of judgment of which the Bible speaks is also described sometimes as a day of 'wrath'.

Many people are understandably worried about describing the reaction of a loving God in this way. It seems to smack of loss of temper or vindictiveness. It appears to be a more appropriate way to describe an angry pagan deity than the God and Father of our Lord Jesus Christ. It is, of course, a word which, like most words, may convey more than one meaning, and which at best is only a partial glimpse into the meaning of a profound truth about God's character.

Certainly, when the Bible speaks of the wrath of God the ideas of vindictiveness, loss of temper, *etc.*, are totally absent. When we speak of 'righteous indignation' we are getting nearer to the idea that anger may be justified and not incompatible with love. When we hear of senseless bombing, or some other act of violence, we can appreciate the need for justice to be done, for wrongdoing to be punished, and for the criminals involved to be helped to live a new life.

It should not surprise us, then, if the source of all moral order demonstrates love and justice together. For to be consistent with his own character, God's love could never be at the expense of his justice.

This, then, is the dilemma. Man was made to enjoy fellowship with God. But somehow all the evidence points to the fact that he has forfeited that privilege. Instead of enjoying God's friendship, he finds himself under the condemnation and 'wrath' of a loving but holy God. We must now turn to see why this should be.

Further reading

God's greatness: Acts 17: 22–34.
God's love: Psalm 78: 38; Jeremiah 31: 3; John 17: 24; 15: 12–15.
God's holiness: Isaiah 6: 1–5; John 4: 1–30; Hebrews 12: 29; 1 John 1: 5.
God's righteous indignation: Romans 1: 18 ff.

What is wrong with man?

There are few people today who would insist on the essential goodness of human nature, as so many pre-war humanists did. On the contrary, many people would agree with Sir Winston Churchill's estimate of man. Speaking in the House of Commons on 28 March 1950 he said, 'Man in this moment of his history has emerged in greater supremacy over the forces of nature than has ever been dreamed of before. He has it in his power to solve quite easily the problem of natural existence. He has conquered the wild beasts, and he has even conquered the insects and the microbes. There lies before him, if he wishes, a golden age of peace and progress. All is in his hand. He has only to conquer his last and worst enemy – *himself.*'

It is still true that we live in an age of boundless possibilities, of great technological progress, national wealth, and educational opportunity for increasing numbers of people. Yet man's inhumanity to man is often as terrible as ever, and man still has within him those evil tendencies that led to the murder of Jesus of Nazareth. There is darkness in man. There is a selfish bias within him. Jesus himself had taught this when he said, 'From the inside, from a man's heart, come the evil ideas which lead him to do immoral things, to rob, kill, commit adultery, covet, and do all sorts of evil things.'

Because man is like this by nature, we should not suppose

that this makes him less responsible for his evil actions. Jesus treated people as morally responsible. 'Why do you call me "Lord, Lord," and don't do what I tell you?' he once exclaimed. And when the apostle Paul spoke about the wrath of God being revealed from heaven against all ungodliness and wickedness in men, he went on to say about these same men that their 'evil ways prevent the truth from being known. . . . So they have no excuse at all!'

A little later in the same passage he says, 'They know that God's law says that people who live in this way deserve death. Yet they continue to do these very things – and worse still, approve of others who do them also.' In the Bible the darkness of man's nature and deeds are described as 'sin', and it is time we examined this important but unpopular word.

What 'sin' means

There are a number of different Greek words in the New Testament that are translated 'sin' which bring out different aspects of the meaning of the word.

1. Man is a law-breaker. Some years ago a man talked with me about his complete lack of any sense of need of God. I remember reminding him of the Ten Commandments and asking him whether he had kept them all. At first he said he had. But when I mentioned to him the fact that Jesus summed up the Ten Commandments in the greatest commandments of all, 'You must love the Lord your God with all your heart, and with all your soul, and with all your mind, and with all your strength' and 'You must love your neighbour as yourself,' he began to realize his need for the forgiveness of sin. He had, like all of us, broken God's greatest commandments.

Sin is breaking God's law. It is directed against God and our fellow-man. It is disobedience.

2. Man is a failure. The verb 'to sin' was sometimes used in classical Greek to mean 'to fall short', with reference to, for example, hurling a spear short of a target. It was also used in the sense of 'missing the road' and so generally 'to fail to do', or to 'fail in one's purpose'.

Paul once wrote that 'all have sinned and fall short of the glory of God'. God's standard is perfection. God's glory is seen supremely in the perfect life of Jesus. None of us would claim that we have lived completely up to our own standards, let alone to those of Jesus Christ. So man is a sinner in this sense too. On his own he is a failure. He has missed the road; he has failed to live up to God's standard as expressed in the perfect life of Jesus Christ.

3. Man is a debtor. In one of Paul's letters there is an obvious reference to an IOU agreement whereby a man signed a scroll with his own hand, acknowledging that he owed a debt to some other man. Paul uses this illustration to emphasize that men owe a debt to God, which they themselves can never repay.

We owe God, for example, a debt of gratitude. For we often fail to thank him for the many things in life which we take for granted, and accept as our right. Sometimes we barely acknowledge God's goodness in giving us health and strength, love and friendship, and indeed all that is good and true and beautiful.

A young Christian who is a professional ballet dancer told me of a colleague who claimed to be an atheist. After considerable discussion, the Christian asked his friend whether there were times when he felt particularly 'inspired' while dancing, and when he captured some rare moment of beauty. His friend agreed there were such moments. The Christian dancer then asked, 'Where did this inspiration come from?' 'It was God-given, I suppose,' said his friend, and then realized with a start what he, an atheist, had said!

But even when we acknowledge that all that is beautiful, good and true comes from the hand of God, which of us adequately expresses our gratitude either in word or action ? Not many would agree that we owe God nothing!

Perhaps Pauls' greatest sense of debt, however, rose from his failure to keep God's law. He knew he owed God a debt of obedience which he could not pay. 'Every man . . . is bound (literally, 'is a debtor') to keep the whole law,' he wrote to the Christians in Galatia. Yet he knew that it was impossible always to 'obey everything that is written in the book of the law'. He owed God an obedience which he could not fully give. He owed God a debt of gratitude and obedience which he could not pay. And both the Bible and our conscience tell us that we are all 'in debt' in the same way.

No wonder Jesus taught us to pray, 'Forgive us our debts'!

The consequences of sin

If I break the law of the land, I expect to suffer for it. Likewise if I break the moral law of God, I shall not be surprised at some serious consequences. Here are some of them:

1. Sin leads to guilt. According to the Bible there is such a thing as moral guilt. Our conscience bears witness to that, as Paul confirms in describing many of his own day who had ignored the law of God: 'Their consciences also show that this is true, since their thoughts sometimes accuse them and sometimes defend them.'

Mind you, there is a difference between *being* guilty and *feeling* guilty. Consider a modern analogy. A man may infringe the Highway Code and break the law of the land without *feeling* guilty at all. Another person may *feel* guilty at the mere sight of a policeman, even though he has done nothing wrong at the time. The man who has broken the law is guilty whether he feels it or not.

Whether or not we *feel* guilty, we *are* morally guilty whenever we break God's laws. And, as one New Testament writer put it, 'whoever breaks only one commandment of the Law is guilty of breaking them all'. Sin deserves judgment.

And since all men are sinners, all stand guilty before a holy God.

2. Sin leads to estrangement. When Jesus told the story of the prodigal son who chose to go his own way and turn his back on his father's home and love, he pictured this man as 'estranged' and 'lost'. Jesus also pictured man as a lost sheep who has gone his own way, or a lost coin which no longer fulfils any useful purpose in life.

A friend of mine once described his attitude to God before he became a Christian. 'I treated God as a stranger,' he said. But others have told me how they rebelled against God, and were hostile towards him. Whether through indifference or hostility, man's attitude to God leads to estrangement, and the need to be brought together, to be reconciled.

3. Sin leads to slavery. For, as Jesus taught with great perception, 'Everyone who sins is a slave of sin.' When a man seeks to live his life without reference to God, he is not as free as he supposes. We have all met those who have become slaves to their selfish desires, whether it be for sex, for money, or for success.

Even the apostle Paul had to admit to knowing the experiences of frustration when he wrote, 'I am mortal man, sold as a slave to sin. I do not understand what I do; for I don't do what I would like to do, but instead I do what I hate.' Sin enslaves. Man needs to be set free to live.

4. Sin leads to death and defeat. In the Bible man's great enemy is death. But 'death' implies more than the disintegration of the body, or the end of physical life. It often means a state of separation from God which it is possible to experience even when we are physically alive.

When Paul, for example, was writing to the Christians at Ephesus, he reminded them of that time before they became Christians, when they were, as he put it, 'spiritually dead because of your disobedience and sins'.

Just as a corpse is unable to respond to outside stimuli,

so they were unable, in their own strength and by their own wisdom, to respond to God. To be dead 'spiritually' is to be unaware of the truth about Jesus. It is to be blind to spiritual truth, and insensitive to spiritual realities. Prayer is meaningless, the Bible irrelevant, worship a mere formality. God himself seems far away, remote, even 'dead'. When the New Testament says, 'Sin pays its wage – death,' it means that here and now a man is spiritually cut off from God.

What about spiritual death? The New Testament teaches that it is appointed to men to die once, and after this comes judgment. Furthermore, Jesus said, 'Do not be afraid of those who kill the body but cannot kill the soul; rather be afraid of God, who can destroy both body and soul in hell.' So it is not physical death that we need to fear, but the consequences of God's judgment on sin. This is called in one place in the New Testament 'the second death'. This phrase, and terms such as 'hell', 'eternal torment', 'darkness' and 'eternal destruction' all speak of the awful possibility of man's final separation from God.

This, then, is man's predicament. How can he escape the guilt, estrangement, slavery, defeat and death that is the consequence of sin? Or we may put this from God's point of view and ask, How can a holy God of love both judge sin and accept and save the sinner?

It is in answer to these questions that the New Testament claim that Jesus came 'to seek and to save the lost' makes sense. He came 'to save sinners' and in order to accomplish that saving he had to die.

So now we are getting near the crunch issue. His death was not just an act of heroism or an example of love. It accomplished something absolutely unique and important for men as sinners. This was why he insisted that his death was 'a must'. And it is in the light of this fact of men under God's judgment that the cross begins to take on that 'glory' of which the New Testament speaks. We are now in a position to come to grips with this central issue.

Further reading

Man's inner nature: Mark 7: 21.
Man's responsibility for what he does: Luke 6: 46; Romans 1: 18, 20, 32.
The greatest commandments: Mark 12: 30, 31.
Man's failure: Romans 2: 23, RSV; 3: 23; Galatians 3: 10–12; 5: 3, RSV. See also Colossians 2: 14.
Conscience and God's law: Romans 2: 15.
Guilt: James 2: 10.
The lost sheep and the lost coin: Luke 15: 1–10.
The prodigal son: Luke 15: 11–32.
Slaves to sin: John 8: 34; Romans 7: 14, 15.
Sin and death: Matthew 10: 28; Romans 6: 23; Ephesians 2: 1.
Why Jesus came: Luke 19: 10.

What did Jesus' death achieve?

8

Connoisseurs of art know only too well how important it is to examine a beautiful art object from different angles and viewpoints if its full beauty is to be appreciated. This is true whether we are viewing a painting or a brilliant gem.

The New Testament writers describe the achievement of Christ's death in similar fashion. They look at it from many different angles and describe its different facets of truth with a variety of illustrations. Each picture throws some light on the meaning of Jesus' death. In this chapter we shall look briefly at the most important pictures. First there is a picture from the law courts.

A just acquittal

Imagine the scene. The prisoner in the dock has confessed his guilt to a charge that the prosecution has brought against him. The judge prepares to pronounce sentence. In legal terms it is a straightforward decision. In personal terms it is agonizing. For the prisoner who stands before him is someone for whom he has the greatest affection and friendship.

At last the judge pronounces his sentence. The prisoner is found guilty. The just sentence – a heavy fine – is pronounced, and the prisoner begins to make his way from the dock to the prison cell. For he has no way of paying such heavy fine.

Then, suddenly, there is a stir in the court. The judge takes off his robes of office and walks swiftly to his friend. 'You're guilty,' he says, 'but I'll pay the fine. You can go free.'

As far as it goes, that story, which I recall being told as a child, conveys part of the truth about Christ's achievement on the cross. For God is just, and to be consistent with his character he must judge the sinner. But God is also loving, and by paying the price of sin, through the death of Jesus, he has found a way of both judging sin and setting the sinner free. He has done for man what man could not possibly do for himself.

The legal term that the New Testament uses to describe this incredible act of God's love is the verb 'justify'. Because Jesus has taken the consequences of man's disobedience, God, out of sheer love, freely declares those who believe in Jesus 'not guilty' or 'acquitted'. The word 'justify' means to 'put in the clear' or 'in the right', with respect to the law. So the believer's sins are forgiven, and he is pronounced 'not guilty'.

Imagine, then, the relief and peace which is experienced by those who believe in Jesus. They can say with the early Christians, 'There is no condemnation now for those who live in union with Christ Jesus.' We are acquitted!

But there is even more to the word 'justify'. It not only means 'to acquit', but also 'to declare righteous'. The truth is that 'in Jesus', God regards the sinner as possessing the 'righteousness' or 'goodness' of Jesus. Righteousness is 'reckoned' to the believer, or 'put to his account'.

Imagine a poor man on the verge of bankruptcy. He has no money of his own. He has no-one to help him. He has wasted his life. Suddenly he hears of the death of a rich uncle, and discovers he has been left a fortune. In due course this vast sum of money is put to his account because of the death of his uncle. This not only means that he no longer fears the bankruptcy courts. It also means that he is rich with the wealth of another – riches that now belong to him because they have been put to his account through another's death. Riches, moreover, which he has neither earned nor deserved.

So this, too, is part of the amazing picture described in the New Testament words about 'God who declares the guilty to be innocent'. By the death of Jesus, those who believe in him and in the good news of his death and resurrection are 'put in the clear', with respect to the law of God. They are also accounted rich with the goodness of Jesus. Jesus' death makes it possible for God to declare me 'not guilty', and to pronounce me 'righteous' in his sight. 'Not a righteousness of my own,' Paul hastens to add, 'the kind to be gained by obeying the Law,' but 'the righteousness which is given through faith in Christ, the righteousness that comes from God, and is based on faith.'

One other way of putting this astounding truth is to say that when I believe Jesus died and rose again for me, it is as if the 'filthy rags' of my own sinful life are laid upon Jesus, in exchange for the spotless robe of Jesus' goodness. There is a real exchange, and so there is a just acquittal.

Good relations

If a son falls out with his father, disobeys him, offends him, and leaves home against his wishes, it is obvious that good relations can be restored only if there is a genuine reconciliation. The New Testament often speaks of *man's need to be reconciled to God*, his heavenly Father. For, as we have already seen, man has rebelled against God. He has disobeyed God, and offended him. Man is sometimes described as an 'enemy of God'. And, like the prodigal son in the story Jesus told, he has turned his back on his Father, gone his own way and wronged him.

But the really heart-warming truth that the New Testament picture of reconciliation emphasizes is that God does not stand aloof and expect man to make the first move back. God has taken the initiative. 'God was in Christ reconciling the world to himself.' And Jesus, you remember, came to seek and to save those who were lost. Indeed, the picture that Jesus gives of God's love is of a waiting father looking out for his returning son, and running out to meet him and to welcome him back home. God has come more than half way to meet us. For God commended his love to us so that 'it was while we were still sinners – enemies – that Christ died for us'.

Of course, sinner man has his part to play if good relations with God are to be restored. 'Be reconciled to God,' urged Paul. But it is God who has made the first move. 'All this is from God, who through Christ reconciled us to himself.'

Now this adds another dimension to the previous truth about God acquitting us because of the death of Jesus. It tells us that God is willing and longing to restore us to a warm, personal relationship with himself, which was his original intention for man. But reconciliation between people normally means a change on both sides. In our analogy it is not only the child who needs to be reconciled to the father. The father also needs to be reconciled to the child. For he has been offended; his rules have been flouted; and if lasting good relations are to be restored the cause of the hostility and rebellion must be fully dealt with, and not glossed over.

According to the New Testament, man's sin offends the holy love of God and, although he never ceases to love us, he cannot restore us to favour and to fellowship with himself unless the cause of the hostility is dealt with. It is not enough that man says he is sorry and returns to God. God has to deal with that which offends his holy love.

This is what the death of Jesus made possible, for although Jesus did not sin, 'God condemned sin' in him. Or, in these amazing words of the apostle Paul, 'God caused Christ, who himself knew nothing of sin, actually to be sin for our sakes, so that in Christ we might be made good with the goodness of God.' So, by his death, Jesus bore God's judgment upon our sin.

But why did Jesus have to suffer?

Why did it have to be Jesus?

Some people have accused Christians of teaching an immoral doctrine about God saving man by punishing an innocent third party, Jesus. Now there would be some force in this accusation if the New Testament teaching about the deity of Jesus was not so strong. But once we accept the claim that Jesus is God, then there is no question of God acting unjustly. The judge and the victim are one. As the apostle Paul wrote, '*God was in Christ* reconciling the world to himself.' It is 'God in Christ' who suffers on the cross.

Such an astonishing truth also answers those who say that if there is a God, he must be remote and unfeeling, because he appears to do little about human suffering. Sidney Carter expressed the view of some, when he wrote:

> 'But God is up in heaven,
> And he doesn't do a thing,
> With a million angels watching,
> And they never move a wing. . . .
> It's God they ought to crucify
> Instead of you and me,
> I said to this Carpenter
> A-hanging on the tree.'

If the Carpenter *is* God, then God is not unfeeling. Far from it. He has entered our world. He has suffered. He has died an agonizing death on a Roman gibbet. His heart has been broken for the sin and suffering of mankind. Above all, he has demonstrated his great love for sinners, bearing their sin and so making possible good relations with himself.

But such love is costly. As we turn now to two further pictures that describe the achievement of Christ's death, we shall consider just how costly it was for God to be in Christ reconciling the world with himself.

Further reading

Our acquittal: Romans 8: 1.
Made righteous: Romans 4: 5; Philippians 3: 9.
Reconciled to God: Romans 5: 8; 2 Corinthians 5: 18–21, RSV.

What is the cost?

9

It should already be clear that there is nothing weak and sentimental about the love of God for sinners. God's love for us is sacrificial and costly. One of the New Testament pictures that most clearly emphasizes this is that which describes the achievement of Jesus' death as a costly ransom.

A costly ransom

Today our newspapers are full of stories of hijacking and kidnapping. We read that a group of desperate men holds a government to ransom. They demand the release of political prisoners in exchange for the lives of innocent passengers aboard a hijacked airliner. Or a group of men kidnap the son of millionaire and demand thousands of pounds as ransom price before they will set him free.

The words 'ransom' and 'redeem' are also to be found in reference to the death of Jesus in the New Testament. To 'redeem' literally means to 'buy back' or 'to pay a price' to set a man free. The price is called a ransom price. Sometimes a slave might be redeemed and set free from slavery, if someone could be found to pay the price of his freedom. Sometimes, in the Old Testament, a man could even be redeemed from a sentence of death. So the New Testament teaches us that Jesus' death is the costly act that sets us free from the consequences of our sin and disobedience.

Jesus said himself that he came into the world 'to give his life as a ransom for many'. And it was one of his close friends, the apostle Peter, who reminded the early Christians just how costly the price was. 'You were ransomed', he said, ' . . . not with perishable things such as silver or gold, but with the precious blood of Christ.'

How costly was Jesus' death?

The cost

There was, of course, the *physical* suffering he endured. We have already noticed the reticence of the New Testament writers to dwell on this aspect of his suffering. But the flogging and the crucifixion itself must have involved terrible physical pain and suffering. The cry 'I am thirsty', gasped from Jesus' lips as he hung naked on that Roman cross, is a tiny hint of what he was suffering on the physical level. Jesus understands physical suffering.

There was also the *mental* suffering that, misunderstood and let down by his friends, Jesus must have suffered. There are few sadder words in the New Testament about Jesus' friends than those that describe their attitude when Jesus was arrested in the Garden of Gethsemane: 'All the disciples left him and ran away.' Jesus understands loneliness.

But, as someone has said, undoubtedly the soul of his sufferings was the sufferings of his soul – that is his *spiritual* suffering. We catch a glimpse of what this meant to Jesus when we see him in the Garden of Gethesemane a few hours before his death. We read that his sweat was like drops of blood falling to the ground. 'Father!' he prayed, 'All things are possible for you. Take this cup away from me. But not what I want, but what you want.'

We hear it again as, hanging on the cross, he cries out, 'My God, my God, why did you abandon me?' Probably Jesus is identifying himself with first the writer of these words, the Psalmist, and with all sinners in speaking of God-forsakenness. He is crying the sinner's cry, for sin separates God from man. He is dying the sinner's death. For a holy God must punish sin. The darkness that came over the earth seems to symbolize the breaking of that fellowship with his Father which he has enjoyed from all eternity.

But for Jesus the costliness of such an experience is all the greater because he is sinless, and is bearing the sin of others. He did no sin. He was the one perfect man that ever lived. As the New Testament writers put it, 'For Christ also died for sins once for all, the righteous for the unrighteous, that he might bring us to God,' 'Christ was without sin, but God made him share our sin,' 'Christ himself carried our sins on his body to the cross.'

If we find it hard to suffer for something we have not done, how costly was it for Jesus to suffer to bring us to God – 'the righteous for the unrighteous'? If we shrink from close association with evil, how costly was it for Jesus to identify himself with all sinners, and to bear in our place the sin of the world?

We can, of course, never fully grasp the spiritual cost of Calvary. But we can catch a glimpse of the greatness of God's love as we remember that Jesus gave his life as 'a *ransom* for many'. For *God* was in Christ.

But the costliness of Jesus' death is not to be understood only with respect to his bearing our sin. It also relates to fighting the powers of evil, and of death itself. For the death of Jesus is also described as a 'victory'.

A decisive victory

In the first century, when a Roman general had won a particularly decisive victory, he was allowed to march his victorious armies through the streets of Rome. Behind them followed the wretched band of prisoners, stripped of their weapons, defeated and powerless. Sometimes Paul thought of Jesus as a triumphant conqueror, enjoying a kind of cosmic triumph. His death on the cross was not defeat, but a decisive victory over the forces of evil. Because of that victory on the cross, the followers of Jesus share in that triumph. They are on the winning side, and the power of evil can never finally defeat them. The forces of evil have been stripped of their ultimate power. 'On that cross Christ freed himself from the power of the spiritual rulers and authorities; he made a public spectacle of them by leading them as captives in his victory procession.'

In recent years in Britain there has been a growing awareness of the power of evil and of evil spirits. Interest in spiritism and the occult has grown. It has been estimated recently that there are something like 2,500 practising witches in Britain alone. People I know of who have started dabbling with spiritism and the occult have later found themselves gripped by fear and powers of evil beyond their control.

In such situations, the victory of Christ's death on the cross is still relevant today. Prayer in the name of Jesus has brought deliverance, just as the apostle John wrote in the book of Revelation about the early Christians: 'Our brothers won the victory over him (Satan) by the blood of the Lamb, and by the truth which they proclaimed; and they were willing to give up their lives and die.'

But let us be clear that such a decisive victory over the forces of evil is not won except at great cost. Once again, perhaps we can begin to understand the cost when we remember Jesus' agony in the Garden of Gethsemane or hear him cry out, 'My God, my God, why did you abandon me?' For Jesus' victory came only through suffering and death. For us victory over evil can come only through faith in the crucified and victorious Jesus whom God raised from the dead.

So by his death Jesus achieved for sinners a just acquittal and good relations between God and men. By his death he paid the price to set man free from the guilt and power of sin, and won a decisive victory over the powers of evil.

How he achieved this we shall see perhaps more clearly when we consider certain Old Testament ideas that throw further light on the meaning of his death.

Further reading

The ransom: Matthew 20: 28, RSV; 1 Peter 1: 18, RSV.
Jesus in Gethsemane: Mark 14: 32–42, 50.
Jesus on the cross: Mark 15: 33–37 (compare Psalm 22: 1); John 19: 28–30.
Jesus' sinlessness: 2 Corinthians 5: 21; 1 Peter 2: 24; 3: 18, RSV.
Jesus' victory: Colossians 2: 15; Revelation 12: 11.

What kind of sacrifice?

10

At times of economic crisis we usually hear the call of politicians urging us to be willing to make sacrifices for the sake of the nation. By this they sometimes mean that we should accept a lower standard of living for a time, or use less electricity in our homes, or cut down on our petrol consumption, or some such action of self-denial.

When we refer to 'sacrifices' today, we are usually thinking of sacrificial actions such as those of the men who laid down their lives in the wars. Or we may speak of the financial sacrifice that parents make for their children, or the sacrifice of professional advantage that a young man may make by opting to give the best years of his life to working in a poor developing country.

We have moved a long way from the meaning of the word 'sacrifice' in the Bible, especially as seen in the Old Testament. When the Old Testament speaks of 'sacrifice' it almost always refers to the sacrifice of animals, which was an important part of the ritual of Jewish religion. It is clear from the New Testament references to the Old Testament sacrifices that they were a preparation for the coming of Jesus the Messiah. According to the New Testament writers, the Old Testament sacrifices were to be compared and contrasted with the death of Jesus.

Sacrifice and 'atonement'

At first sight it may seem strange that there can be any comparison between the slaughter of animals in Jewish religious history and the meaning of the death of Jesus, the Son of God. Indeed, many would heartily agree with one modern writer who has stated, 'The modern layman can well do without St Paul's obsession about sin, and the imagery of being washed in blood.'

But it is impossible to divorce the history of the Old Testament from the life, death and resurrection of Jesus. For Jesus was born a Jew of Jewish parentage. He fulfilled the Jewish law in detail. He understood his own mission in the light of the Old Testament Scriptures. In particular, he believed that the Scriptures could be fulfilled only by his death. He expected his disciples to understand his death in this way too. 'Was it not necessary for the Messiah to suffer these things and enter his glory?' he said to two friends on a walk on the Emmaus road. 'And Jesus explained to them what was said about him in all the Scriptures, beginning with the books of Moses and the writings of all the prophets.'

So Jesus believed that the Old Testament Scriptures could throw light on the meaning of his mission, and especially of his death. We see this most clearly when we compare the ritual sacrifice of animals with the death of Jesus, whom the New Testament sometimes calls 'the Lamb of God'.

The Old Testament is full of instructions about the way to get right with God. We read in one Old Testament passage, for example: 'If any one of the common people sins . . . If he brings a lamb as his offering for a sin offering, he shall bring a female without blemish, and lay his hand upon the head of the sin offering, and kill it . . . Then the priest shall take some of the blood of the sin offering with his finger and put it on the horns of the altar of burnt offering, and pour out the rest of its blood at the base of the altar . . . and the priest shall make atonement for him for the sin which he has committed, and he shall be forgiven.'

If we read these words carefully we notice that the sacrifice of an animal and the shedding of blood had something to do with 'atonement'. This word literally means *at-one-ment*, or being made 'at one' with God. As we have already seen, man's sin and disobedience offend the holy God of love, so that man cannot be 'at one' with God unless the offence is dealt with. But the story of the Bible is the story of this very God, whom we have offended, providing a way for the offence to be dealt with, first ceremonially through the sacrifice of animals, and then actually through the sacrifice of Jesus, the Lamb of God. God provided the sacrifice. God was in Christ. God's honour was satisfied by Jesus' death.

The 'blood of the covenant'

Sacrifice and 'atonement' are also at the root of another important theme in the Old Testament – the covenant. We are familiar today with 'deeds of covenant' and similar agreements and contracts. In the Bible, God's special relationship with his people is described as a 'covenant' or solemn agreement. The book of Exodus describes in some detail how God entered into a covenant with his chosen people in the days of Moses.

First God spoke to Moses and Moses gave to the people 'all these words which the Lord had commanded him'. Then the people responded to God's initiative by solemnly promising, 'All that the Lord has spoken we will do.' Finally, as a symbol of atonement and cleansing, the sacrifices were offered, and the blood of the sacrificed animals was sprinkled on the altar and then upon the people as they committed themselves to obey God.

How does this throw light on Jesus' death? When he spoke to his disciples on the eve of his crucifixion, he told them that his death would make possible a 'new covenant' with God. In Old Testament days, the prophets Jeremiah and Ezekiel had foreseen this and spoken of a 'new covenant'. 'I will put my law within them, and I will write it upon their hearts; . . . they shall all know me, from the least of them to the greatest, says the Lord; for I will forgive them their iniquity, and I will remember their sin no more.'

The 'blood of the covenant' in the Old Testament, then, is a vivid reminder that forgiveness of sins and a personal relationship with God is impossible apart from sacrifice. When Jesus spoke about his death to his disciples on the evening before he was crucified, he endorsed this by saying, 'This is my blood, which seals God's covenant, my blood, poured out for many for the forgiveness of sins.' The death of Jesus made possible a new covenant with God, a relationship in which the assurance of forgiveness, and the desire and power to do God's will, are most certainly realities.

I was travelling in a train from Edinburgh to London when I became involved in a conversation with an orthodox Jew. In the course of our discussion I asked him what he thought of the Old Testament promises of the new covenant. He told me that such promises would, he believed, be fulfilled when the Messiah came. 'Our rabbi tells us', he said, 'that now it is difficult to keep God's law. It is a struggle. We have no inward strength. But then it will be easier for we shall have his power within us.' I told him that Christians were convinced that the Messiah had come, and that the death of Jesus made possible a 'new covenant', or a new relationship, with God which brought forgiveness and inner strength to all who believed.

But these Old Testament examples not only remind us of the necessity for sacrifice if man's sin is to be forgiven and 'atonement' achieved. They also illustrate the way in which Jesus' death makes this possible. For clearly the animal that is killed dies in place of the sinner who deserves death. The Lamb is a substitute for the sinner.

Take, for example, the famous Jewish feast of the Passover. At the feast every Jew was, and still is today, reminded of the way in which God had rescued the Hebrews from the slavery of Egypt in the days of Moses.

The feast of the Passover was commemorated in Old Testament times by the slaying of a lamb. For God said that by putting the blood of the lamb upon the door-posts of the Hebrew homes, the first-born son would be saved from the judgment of death. In this story, the angel of death *passed over* every household covered by the blood of the lamb. In other words, the lamb died in place of the eldest son in the Hebrew family.

Or think of the ritual on the Day of Atonement. On this day the high priest offered a bull to atone for the sins of the priests. Then he took the blood into the innermost part of the Temple and offered it to God. Next he took the blood of a goat and offered it for the sins of the nation. Finally, the high priest confessed the sins of the nation in the presence of the people, placing his hands on the head of a second goat.

But then notice what happened: this second goat was led into the wilderness and left to die. It was in fact a 'scapegoat' – a word we still use today. Thus it was a constant reminder to the Jew that if a man was to escape God's just judgment, another must bear the consequences of sin in his place.

This truth is further endorsed by the frequent use of the word 'blood' with reference to sacrificial death. Normally 'the blood' refers to 'the life laid down'. It is evidence that death has taken place. It also frequently refers to the idea that the life is laid down in exchange for or in place of another.

A story is told of Charles Simeon, an eighteenth-century vicar, who became well known for his ministry at Holy Trinity Church, Cambridge. When he was a student at King's College, he was summoned to attend a compulsory service of Holy Communion on Easter Sunday. The summons caused him a great deal of consternation and heart-searching, for he had no first-hand knowledge of God, and he felt totally unready to attend a service of this kind. In the course of his reading, however, he came across a reference to the Old Testament sacrifices and the way they illustrated the meaning of the death of Christ. Writing about this later he said, 'As I was reading . . . I met with an expression to this effect – "That the Jews knew what they did, when they transferred their sin to the head of their offering." The thought came into my mind, What, may I transfer all my guilt to another? Has God provided an Offering for me, that I may lay my sins in His head? Then, God willing, I will not bear them on my own soul one moment longer. Accordingly I sought to lay my sins upon the sacred head of Jesus.'

For Simeon, then, the chief lesson he learnt from the comparison of Old Testament sacrifices with the death of Jesus was that they helped him to see that Jesus' death was in the place of sinners. It was John the Baptist who pointed to Jesus and said, 'Here is the Lamb of God who takes away the sin of the world!' It was the apostle Peter who wrote, 'Christ himself carried our sins in his body to the cross.' Jesus' death was a perfect sacrifice. Jesus is the perfect substitute. I deserved to die. He died in my place.

There is a further obvious comparison. The sacrificial animal, for example the Passover lamb, was often required to be 'without spot or blemish'. Jesus could take away the sins of the world by his sacrificial death only because he too was 'without spot or blemish'. That is, although he was tempted in all points as we are, yet it was without sin. He did no sin. He was 'separate from sinners'. He led a life of perfect obedience.

The 'suffering Servant'

In one Old Testament book there is an important development of this idea of a spotless sacrificial lamb becoming a substitute for sinners, an idea which seems to have influenced Jesus' understanding of his death, and his disciples' interpretation of it. In the book of Isaiah we are introduced to

68

a 'Servant of the Lord' whose lot it will be to represent the people and innocently to suffer for them. His suffering is like that of 'a lamb that is led to the slaughter, and like a sheep that before its shearers is dumb'.

In a remarkable anticipation of Jesus' own sufferings, Isaiah tells us that the Servant of the Lord 'was despised and rejected by men; a man of sorrows and acquainted with grief . . . he was despised, and we esteemed him not'. But it is in Isaiah's description of the suffering Servant innocently bearing the sins of others that we find the most startling comparison with Jesus' death: 'Surely he has borne our griefs and carried our sorrows; yet we esteemed him stricken, smitten by God, and afflicted. But he was wounded for *our* transgressions, he was bruised for *our* iniquities; upon him was the chastisement that made *us* whole, and with his stripes we are healed.'

Then Isaiah sums up the significance of Jesus' death in a nutshell. 'All we like sheep have gone astray; we have turned every one to his own way; and *the Lord has laid on him* the iniquity of us all.' Jesus certainly identified himself with this suffering Servant. For example, he once said to his disciples, 'The scripture that says, "He was included with the criminals," must come true about me.'

The apostles came to understand his death in these terms. 'When he was cursed he did not answer back with a curse; when he suffered he did not threaten, but placed his hopes in God, the righteous judge. Christ himself carried our sins on his body to the cross, so that we might die to sin and live for righteousness. By his wounds you have been healed. You were like sheep that had lost their way.' Peter is quoting almost exactly from Isaiah and applying these words to Jesus.

So Jesus is the suffering Servant who was wounded for us, and died, 'the righteous for the unrighteous, to bring us to God'.

Contrasts

The New Testament writers had no doubt at all that Jesus' sacrifice on the cross was a unique and final sacrifice. There are certainly comparisons between the Old Testament sacrifices and the sacrificial death of Jesus. But the contrasts between the animal sacrifices of the Old Testament and the perfect sacrifice of Jesus stand out still more clearly. Here are some of them.

1. Jesus' sacrifice really did take away sins, whereas, as the Christian writer to the Hebrews expressed it, 'the blood of bulls and goats can never take sins away'. In the animal sacrifice there is a reminder of sin; in the death of Jesus there is the forgiveness of sins. As the same writer put it, 'he has now appeared once and for all, when all the ages of time are nearing their end, to remove sin through the sacrifice of himself'.

It does not matter how greatly a man has sinned; it is still true that 'the blood of Jesus goes on cleansing from all sin'. As an Old Testament writer poetically expressed it, 'As far as the east is from the west, so far has God set our sin from us.'

Through Jesus' sacrifice there is a complete 'wiping of the slate clean'; there is complete, full and free forgiveness. We might say of someone who has wronged us, 'I could never forgive him for that.' But on the basis of Jesus' death, the early Christians knew that 'if we confess our sins to God, we can trust him, for he does what is right – he will forgive our sins and make us clean from *all* our wrong-doing'. Or again, we might say, 'I can never forget what wrong he did me,' but God says, 'I will not remember their sins and wicked deeds any longer.'

2. Jesus' sacrifice was once and for all, whereas, quoting again from the letter to the Hebrews, 'the sacrifices serve to remind people of their sins, year after year'.

The writer goes on, 'Every Jewish priest stands and performs his services every day and offers the same sacrifices many times. But these sacrifices can never take away sins. Christ, however, offered one sacrifice for sins, an offering that is good for ever, and then sat down at the right side of God. . . . So when these (sins) have been forgiven, an offering to take away sins is no longer needed.'

In other words, the sacrifices of the Old Testament foreshadowed and pointed towards the once-and-for-all sacrifice of Jesus Christ upon the cross. Once Jesus had shed his blood there was no further need for the shedding of the blood of animals. It is an interesting thought that after the destruction of the Temple in AD 70, the Jews no longer offered animal sacrifices as they had always done previously. Christians recognize that Christ's death was once and for all. It was a perfect and sufficient sacrifice. It needs no repetition.

3. Jesus' sacrifice had eternal consequences, whereas the Old Testament sacrifices had only temporary value. The temporary value was of a ceremonial and preparatory kind. But the same writer to the Hebrews tells that Christ's death was 'one sacrifice . . . that is good *for ever*', and that Jesus' offer of himself obtained eternal benefits.

No wonder the early Christians had a new confidence in prayer and a new joy in worship. There was no longer the need for countless sacrifices to be made. Access to God's presence was no longer confined to the high priest and the privileged few. Jesus was seen to be the perfect high priest and also to have offered in himself the one perfect and sufficient sacrifice for the sins of the whole world.

When Jesus was dying on the cross at Calvary, a remarkable incident took place. It was said that the great curtain that separated the Holy of Holies from the rest of the Temple was torn from top to bottom, as if by an invisible hand, as Jesus cried out 'Finished!' just before he died.

Whether or not such an incident was caused by an earth tremor, it symbolized perfectly the meaning of Christ's sacrifice on the cross. Christ's sacrifice had made a way into God's presence possible for everyone who believes.

'We have, then,' wrote the writer of the letter to the Hebrews, 'complete freedom to go into the Most Holy Place by means of the death of Jesus. He opened for us a new way, a living way, through the curtain – that is, through his own body. . . . Let us come near to God, then, with a sincere heart and a sure faith, with hearts that have been made clean from a guilty conscience.'

That is perfectly possible. For Jesus' death was a perfect and sufficient sacrifice. Jesus is our perfect substitute.

There is one further picture of Jesus' death that sums up much of what we have already said about his achievement. It is contained in the word 'salvation', or its more modern counterpart 'liberation'. It is this that must concern us in the following chapter.

Further reading

Jesus speaks of his death: Luke 24: 13–35.
Old Testament sacrifices for atonement: Leviticus 4: 27–35.
God's covenant with Moses: Exodus 19: 1 onwards.
The Old Testament looks forward to the 'new covenant': Jeremiah 31: 31–34; Ezekiel 36: 22–32.
Jesus and the 'new covenant': Matthew 26: 26–28.
The first passover: Exodus 12: 21–27.
The scapegoat: Leviticus 16: 20–22.
Jesus' sacrifice: John 1: 29; 1 Peter 2: 24.
The Servant of the Lord: Isaiah 42–53; see especially 53: 3–12 (compare Luke 22: 37; 1 Peter 3: 18, RSV).
Jesus' sacrifice removes sin: Hebrews 9: 26; 10: 4, 17 (compare Psalm 103: 2); 1 John 1: 7–9.
Jesus' sacrifice once for all: Hebrews 10: 3, 11–18.
Rending of the curtain: Mark 15: 38; Hebrews 10: 19–22.

H. G. C. Moule's *Charles Simeon* is published by IVP (1965). The passage quoted is from pages 25, 26.

Complete liberation?

11

The twentieth century certainly does not lack liberation movements. Throughout the world there are numerous groups of men, sometimes desperate, who set out to rescue and deliver their own people from supposed injustice, slavery, and oppression. Nearer home we have Students' Lib, Gay Lib and Women's Lib!

In this respect, as in others, the Bible remains an astonishingly up-to-date and relevant book. It is the story of a great liberation movement. God is the liberator, and the Bible is the story of the way in which he set out to liberate or 'save' his people.

Salvation—liberation

'Salvation' is a word that is often used in the Bible. But it is important to realize that it is often used in the broadest sense of the term.

When God 'saved' Israel from the Egyptians in the days of Moses, he saved them from *slavery*.

When the Psalmist spoke about salvation, he often referred to God's activity in saving his people from poverty, injustice, and hunger.

When Jesus came to seek and to save those who were lost, he included as part of his mission the healing of the sick, the restoring of sight to the blind, and the preaching of good news to the poor. He cared about people as a whole – body and soul.

I read recently the rather delightful story of a young Negro Pentecostal from New York who gathered his congregation one evening for what he called a hand-clapping, foot-stamping, earth-shaking prayer meeting at the entrance of a large department store. The management at this store, although relying on black custom, was mean over the employment and promotion of blacks. When the assistant manager approached the Christians, offering to negotiate, the young minister had replied, 'Man, I'm talking to the Lord. Either talk to the Lord or get out of my way,' and they went on praying for the soul of the manager. Next day the store opened up a whole range of new jobs for blacks.

God's salvation includes the liberation of the whole man. Man has social and physical as well as spiritual needs. So Christians should be concerned about the whole man – soul and body – and the conditions in which he lives. As we have already seen, however, Jesus died specifically to 'save us from our sins' and the New Testament mostly speaks about salvation in this sense. But here again it is important to notice the full scope of this word.

Some years ago a bishop was travelling in the same compartment as a Salvation Army lass. She leaned forward and asked the bishop earnestly, 'Are you saved, sir?'

The bishop thought for a moment and then said, 'My dear, do you mean *sotheseis*, *sozomenos*, or *sothesomenos*?' The Salvation Army girl replied, 'I asked you a plain question – Are you saved? Can you not give me a plain, straightforward answer?'

The bishop gently reminded her that her question was neither plain nor straightforward. Accordingly he had given her the Greek participles to enable her to be a bit more precise. Her question could mean, he said, 'Have I been saved?' 'Am I being saved?', or 'Do I hope to be saved?' He then went on to tell her how when he was eighteen *he had been saved* – that is, that he knew his sins had been

74

washed away. Furthermore, he was *being saved* that very day, and he had every confidence that *he would be finally saved*, body and soul, because he was sure that the Lord Jesus, who had begun a good work in him, would continue it right through to eternity. The bishop was right. For the New Testament speaks of salvation as being past, present and future.

'We have been saved'

Looking back to the past, the Christian can say that Jesus has saved him from the *penalty* of sin. As we have learnt from the various pictures that throw light on the meaning of Jesus' death, Jesus bore the penalty of sin by his death on the cross. He took our place. He suffered the consequences of sin – not his, but ours. So, 'in Jesus', that is, united by faith to him, there is for us *no condemnation. We have been saved*. We have passed from death into life. We have been transferred from the kingdom of Satan to the kingdom of God's dear Son.

Some people can remember the first time when they trusted in Jesus Christ, and so were 'saved' from the penalty of sin, and became Christians. Other people cannot remember the exact time. They only know that once they were not saved, and now they are. That once they were dead, spiritually, and now they are alive. That once they were blind, and now they see.

Every real Christian looking back to the past can know that he *has been saved*. There is no doubt about that among New Testament Christians.

There is, of course, no ground for boasting in such a claim. For our 'salvation' depends not on what we do for Jesus, but on what he has done for us. Not our 'good deeds' in the world, but his achievement on the cross.

The apostle Paul put it like this: 'It is by God's grace (that is, by his undeserved favour) that *you have been saved*, through faith. *It is not of your own doing*, but God's gift.'

'We are being saved'

One of the disconcerting characteristics of some fine African Christians is the way in which they sometimes ask European Christians about the reality of their Christian experience. They will not only ask, even of senior missionaries, 'Are you saved?', but they will go on to say, 'And how are you today, brother?' In other words, they are rightly concerned not only about salvation in the past, but in the present. They rightly believe that Jesus Christ saves us from the power as well as the penalty of sin.

How does the death of Jesus Christ help us to overcome sin and temptation in the course of everyday living? In what sense does the Christian enjoy the experience of 'being saved'?

1. **Jesus' death saves us from the stain or defilement of sin.** Jesus gave his disciples an unforgettable illustration of this fact during his last supper with them. A man on a day's journey, he said, needs to take a bath only once, but he may need to wash his sandalled feet, dusty from the journey, several times. 'Whoever has taken a bath is completely clean and does not need to wash himself, except for his feet.' In the same way a Christian is 'saved' or 'justified' once. He has been saved from the penalty of sin. But he needs to be saved daily from the defilement of sinning, from the stains of daily wrongdoing.

So the apostle John could write, 'The blood of Jesus . . . makes us clean (or goes on cleansing) from every sin.' Or again, 'If we confess our sins to God, we can trust him, for he does what is right – he will forgive us our sins and make us clean from all our wrongdoing.'

We recognize in family life the distinction between a 'once-for-all' relationship and a daily fellowship. Nothing can alter the fact of the relationship between parents and their child. But if I wrong my parents and fail to apologize, although the fact of the relationship remains, the fellowship and friendship and enjoyment of the relationship is marred. It can be put right only when I have apologized and said 'sorry'.

Once I have become a Christian I have been saved and I do not need to become a Christian all over again. But I do need to say 'sorry' when I let God down, if I am to enjoy fellowship with him. When I do this, the benefits of Jesus' death are always available. 'The blood of Jesus goes on cleansing.'

2. Jesus' death sets us free from the slavery of sin.

For, as Jesus said, 'Everyone who sins is a slave of sin.'

There is an interesting illustration of this in Somerset Maugham's book *Of Human Bondage*. Philip, the chief character in the book, has thrown away his childhood belief in God and his acceptance of Christian moral standards. He expects to discover freedom and liberty in living as he pleases without reference to God. Instead of this, we read, 'Philip was astounded at the weakness of his will. It seemed to him that he was swayed by every high emotion, as though he was a leaf in the wind. And when passion seized him, he was powerless. He had no self-control. He considered with some irony the philosophy which he had developed for himself, for it had not been much use to him. He thought of what he was going to do, and when the time came to act, he was powerless in the grasp of instincts, emotions, he knew not what. His reason was looking on observing the facts, but powerless to interfere.'

The death of Jesus sets us free from such impotence. When the Lilliputians in Swift's famous novel cut the cords that bound Gulliver completely to the ground, they set him free to live among them, and ultimately to return to his own country. They set him *free*. Similarly, the death of Jesus cuts the cords that bind us. The Spirit of the living Lord Jesus then gives the Christian believer both the desire and the power to do God's will, and to enjoy the liberty of the children of God.

Paul wrote to the Christians at Rome, 'But thanks be

God! For at one time you were slaves to sin, but now you obey with all your hearts the truths found in the teaching you received. You were set free from sin and became the slaves of righteousness.' For the death and resurrection of Jesus set the Christian free from the slavery of sin in all its forms – selfishness, discontent, fear, envy, pride, laziness and so on. Paul could say, 'I am no longer a slave of sin, because Jesus' death has set me free.'

'We shall be saved'

Finally, the Christian looks to the future and trusts God to save him from future judgment and for the life of heaven, through the death of Jesus. For by his death Jesus has secured for the believer an 'eternal redemption' of body and soul. There is a 'salvation which is ready to be revealed at the end of time'.

Perhaps the best description of what that means is given by the apostle John when he writes, 'We are now God's children, but it is not yet clear what we shall become. But this we know: when Christ appears, *we shall become like him, because we shall see him as he really is.*'

Let me say again that this confidence in a future salvation does not depend on anything a man has done, but on what Jesus has done for him on the cross. So when Jesus cried out 'Finished!' just before he died, it was a cry of triumph and accomplishment. He had finished the work he had come to do. He had achieved for man what man could not achieve for himself. He had, by his death, made possible man's acceptance, forgiveness, reconciliation, freedom, and final victory over all that sin, the devil and death could do to him. In a word, he had accomplished man's *salvation.*

But how may I personally enjoy the benefits of so great a salvation ? And how should the death of Christ affect my life in the twentieth century ?

Further reading

'*You have been saved*': Ephesians 2: 8.
Being freed from the stain of sin: John 13: 10; 1 John 1: 7, 9.
Being freed from the slavery of sin: John 8: 34; Romans 6:
17, 18.
Future salvation: 1 Peter 1: 5; 1 John 3: 2.

What must I do?

12

Some years ago in the United States of America a man called George Wilson was indicted for robbing a mail van and putting the life of the driver in jeopardy. He was condemned to death. Shortly before his execution, however, he was pardoned by the President. When the warder presented the pardon to the prisoner in his cell, he refused to accept it, saying that he wanted to die. 'Well,' the warder said, 'all right, you will die; we'll go ahead with the execution.' But Wilson's attorney obtained a stay of execution. It was his contention that you could not execute the man: he had been pardoned.

The case was brought to the Supreme Court of the United States. The decision of that Court read as follows: 'A pardon is a deed, to the validity of which delivery is essential; and delivery is not complete without acceptance. It may be then rejected . . . and if it be rejected, we have discovered no power in a court to force it on him. It may be supposed that no one being condemned to death would reject a pardon, but the rule must be the same.' George' Wilson did not accept his pardon, and went to execution by his own choice.

The free pardon and the new life that God offers us, on the basis of the death of Christ, must similarly be accepted. For the New Testament also says that a pardon is valid only if it is accepted. If we ignore or reject it, then we must pay the death penalty ourselves. As the apostle John wrote in his Gospel: 'Whoever believes in the Son has eternal life; whoever disobeys the Son will never have life, but God's wrath will remain on him for ever.'

What, then, must we do to receive the benefits of the death of Jesus?

A few weeks after Jesus had been seen alive from the dead, Peter preached to thousands in the open air in Jerusalem. He spoke to them of the life, death and resurrection of Jesus. He did not hesitate to declare that they were as much responsible for Jesus' death as anyone else. '*You* killed him, by letting sinful men nail him to the cross.'

The climax of Peter's sermon came when he said, 'All the people of Israel, then, are to know for sure that it is this Jesus, whom you nailed to the cross, that God has made Lord and Messiah!' At this many in the crowd became anxious and concerned, and said to Peter and the rest of the apostles, 'What shall we do, brothers?' Peter's answer is for all time: 'Turn away from your sins, each one of you, and be baptized in the name of Jesus Christ, so that your sins will be forgiven; and you will receive God's gift, the Holy Spirit.'

From these words we understand that water baptism was linked with forgiveness and the gift of the Spirit, that is, it was linked with cleansing and new life. These are the gifts given to all who belong to Jesus. So baptism was an outward sign of belonging to Jesus, and thereby to the church. But the New Testament makes it clear that the outward sign of baptism does not automatically bring the inward experience of forgiveness and new life. A man may be baptized in water but not 'baptized in the Spirit', the initial experience of receiving new life.

So Peter calls here for an inward response from his listeners. His call to 'be baptized' was also a call for *inward* repentance, faith and committal. What does this mean?

Repentance

This is an unfashionable word in the twentieth century. It literally means 'a change of mind'. In the Christian sense it implies a change of direction and a change of our way of life. It means both 'feeling sorry' and 'showing that we are sorry'. The prodigal son in Jesus' parable learnt what repentance meant only after he had come to his senses, gone to his father and said, 'Father, I have sinned against God and against you.'

So repentance means that I admit I am a sinner; that I am willing to confess my sins to God and to return to him. It means that I am willing to go his way instead of my own way.

Now we may well see our need to repent when we recognize how often we have broken God's moral law in thought, word and deed. But the New Testament also teaches that there is a sense in which we need to repent for sharing in the rejection and crucifixion of Jesus, by our attitude to him today.

Robert Keable once expressed this movingly when he wrote: 'No little crippled child is born of sin into a world of love in Hoxton, but Jesus drinks again of a cup that may not pass away . . . no maimed or half blind soul is made to stumble somewhere off Piccadilly but a Judas has betrayed his Lord again for a few pieces of silver. No boastful but frightened disciple sits by a fire in Mayfair when Jesus is called in question, and denies Him at the test, but once again that Master is wounded more deeply than by Roman or by Jew, in the house of his friends. And even more, nowhere is deliberate sin planned and performed, but someone has ridden by the Cross on Calvary and stabbed Jesus to the heart.'

How many of us, I wonder, have seen our own sin and failure in the light of Jesus' death? Certainly the jealousy, prejudice and hatred of the religious leaders is not confined to men of the first century. Also many today are guilty of the same weakness, fear and indecision that Pontius Pilate shared when confronted with the challenge of Jesus Christ. And those in the crowd who were so easily led to shout 'Crucify him!' are little different from those who stoop to dishonesty or other malpractices, because 'everybody does it', and so ignore the teaching of Jesus.

Furthermore, the callous indifference of the soldiers, and no doubt of many others in Jerusalem on the day that Jesus died, is familiar enough to the twentieth-century scene. Studdert-Kennedy well expressed it some years ago:

'When Jesus came to Golgotha, they hanged Him on a tree,
They drove great nails through hands and feet and made a calvary.
They crowned Him with a crown of thorns, red were the wounds and deep,
For those were crude and cruel days, and human flesh was cheap.

When Jesus came to Birmingham, they simply passed Him by,
They never hurt a hair of Him, they only let Him die.
For men had grown more tender, and they would not give Him pain,
They only just passed down the street, and left Him in the rain.

Still Jesus cried "Forgive them; for they know not what they do."
And still it rained this wintry rain, that drenched Him through and through.
The crowds went home and left the streets, without a soul to see,
And Jesus crouched against a wall, and cried for Calvary.'

Sometimes it must be our sheer indifference to Jesus that hurts him most.

If, then, I am to receive the benefits of Christ's death, I must be willing to 'repent' of my own sin and failure, both in breaking God's law and in crucifying the Son of God afresh. I must feel sorrow, confess my failure, be willing to forsake my selfish attitudes and my sinful actions, and show that I mean it. Secondly, as well as genuine repentance there must be personal faith in Jesus.

Faith

We can see this from another incident in the New Testament when the prison jailer at Philippi asked the two Christians, Paul and Silas, 'What must I do to be saved?' Paul replied, 'Believe in the Lord Jesus, and you will be saved.' Then the jailer and his household were baptized.

Faith has an *intellectual* element in it. The 'would-be' Christian is asked to believe certain facts about Jesus: that Jesus is the living Lord or God, and that he is 'the Christ', the Messiah or King. Paul would surely have explained that the name 'Jesus' means 'Saviour' or 'Deliverer', and that Jesus came to save the people from their sins, by his death and resurrection.

In a modern baptism service, three important questions are sometimes put to the adult candidate, or to the parents of a child, when a child is baptized:

1. Do you believe and trust in God the Father who made the world?

2. Do you believe and trust in his Son Jesus Christ, who redeemed mankind?

3. Do you believe and trust in his Holy Spirit, who sanctifies (makes holy, distinct and Christlike) the people of God?

What is our response to these questions? Can we give intellectual assent to these essential statements about the Christian faith? That is important. But there is more to faith than intellectual assent to general statements about God. There is a *personal* element in faith.

John Wesley, the eighteenth-century Anglican clergyman, while on his way to America to do missionary work met a group of Moravian Christians on board ship. In his *Journal*,

Wesley records how they asked him whether he believed in Jesus Christ as his personal Saviour. Wesley had said that he believed Jesus was the Saviour of the world. 'But do you believe he saved *you*?' persisted the questioner. Wesley records sadly, 'I said that I did, but I fear they were vain words.' And so, in spite of his years of intellectual faith in God, it was only later, in a room in Aldersgate Street, London, that he records 'an assurance was given me that my sins, even mine, were forgiven'. Only then, it seems, did his faith in Jesus become personal, living and real.

If I am to enjoy the benefits of Jesus' death for myself, then it is not enough to have an intellectual belief in general statements about God, and the Christian faith, important as such a faith is. I must also have a personal trust in Jesus as the God-Man who died for my sins on the cross, and lives to give *me* new life by his Spirit. 'I live by faith in the Son of God, who loved *me* and gave his life for *me*,' wrote Paul about his own Christian experience.

But someone may well ask, how can I be sure that I have a personal and living faith in Jesus? The answer to that question lies in the fact that faith not only has an intellectual and personal element in it, but also a *practical* element. In a word, Christian faith involves commitment.

Commitment

When a girl begins to be attracted to a young man and they discover that their feelings are mutual, there often follows a time of 'mentally' weighing up one another. Indeed, however much the 'heart' is involved, it is certainly wise to let the mind guide us at such times! Similarly, when we begin to be attracted to Jesus Christ and when he makes himself known to us, it is right that we should consider his character and claims, and come to believe that he is a person who can utterly be trusted and loved for time and eternity. For Jesus is alive today, the living Saviour, Master and God, calling us to come to him.

But in our human relationships, the 'mutual attraction' and the 'mental weighing up' would never lead to the union of marriage unless there came a moment of commitment. I have taken part in many wedding services, but I have not yet met any young man or woman who has been unwilling to say these two words of commitment 'I will' to the one they love.

The New Testament teaches me that if I am to enjoy a new relationship with Jesus, and the benefits of forgiveness and new life that he gives, then I must be willing to commit myself to Jesus as my Saviour and my God. I must do more than 'feel attracted' to him. I must do more than intellectually believe that he is Son of God and Saviour, utterly trustworthy, and loving. I must be willing to say to Jesus, 'I will trust you with all my life and follow you as my Saviour, Master and God.'

For Jesus Christ offers us forgiveness and new life if only we will turn to him in repentance, faith and commitment. God alone can give us the strength to make such a response. But the choice is ours.

Now if I commit myself to Jesus Christ in this way, I need to remember that this commitment is only the beginning of a new relationship. A married couple need to make time and to take the trouble to enrich and develop their relationship with one another. It is equally true that a Christian needs to take time and trouble to develop his relationship with Jesus.

Once he is committed to Jesus Christ he will discover the importance of spending time with Jesus, talking to him in prayer and listening to him as he reads and thinks about God's message in the Bible. He will want to spend time with God's family, the church, and to honour him in worship, and in service in the world. And the fact is that once he is committed to Jesus, he will experience the Spirit of Jesus in him, giving him a new desire to know him, and make him better known.

In addition, a Christian finds that Jesus' love for him, revealed supremely in his death on the cross, can be a constant inspiration and incentive for living the Christian life. That must be the theme for the final chapter of this book.

Further reading

Accepting Jesus' forgiveness: John 3: 36.
Peter's speech after Jesus' resurrection: Acts 2: 14–40, especially verses 23, 36–38.
The prodigal son: Luke 15: 11–32.
The Philippian jailer: Acts 16: 30, 31.
Paul's faith: Galatians 2: 20.

The story of George Wilson is quoted from the Fact and Faith booklet *Red River of Life* by Dr Irwin Moon. According to Moon, the case may be found in the United States Supreme Court Reports, Peters, volume 7. The case is United States v. George Wilson.

For love of Jesus

13

Most of us freely acknowledge our need for incentives to get the best out of us. The student will work all the harder if there's the prospect of a 'first'; the games player, if he can represent his country; the research student, if he can obtain a doctorate; the businessman, tradesman, industrial worker or professional man, if there is a prospect of a rise, or promotion, or some improvement to his quality of life.

But it is also true to say that one of man's greatest incentives still is love. Some people will give their lives for love of their country, or for some cause they regard as important. Many a young man has made sacrifices, and even changed his way of life, for love of a girl. And if someone loves us, and makes sacrifices for us, we would be very heartless not to respond with gratitude and love in return.

It is not surprising, therefore, that perhaps the greatest incentive for the early Christians for loving God and for expressing their love in worship, Christian living and Christian service was the love of God revealed in Jesus' death. 'We love', wrote the apostle John, 'because God first loved us.' And by their love they 'turned the world upside down'.

Christian worship

It is hard to visit a church anywhere in the world without

finding somewhere, in a prominent position, the symbol of the cross. Many churches, when they meet together to give God his worth (for that is what worship means), recite together the words: 'Jesus . . . suffered under Pontius Pilate, was crucified, dead and buried . . . and rose again the third day.' And this is intended to be no dull repetition of the facts of the Christian story, but a constant reminder of the love of God revealed in Jesus, and of the love and gratitude we owe him.

Jesus himself taught the disciples to keep his death before them. It is astonishing in a way that the one 'service' that Jesus instituted was to be primarily a reminder, not of his life and ministry, or of his miracles, or even primarily of his resurrection, but of his death.

For at a Passover meal with his disciples in the evening before he died, Jesus 'took the bread, gave thanks to God, broke it, and gave it to them, saying, "This is my body which is given for you. Do this in memory of me." In the same way he gave them the cup, after the supper, saying, "This cup is God's new covenant sealed with my blood which is poured out for you." ' When Paul wrote to the churches at Corinth describing this event, he added the comment, 'For until the Lord comes, you proclaim his death whenever you eat this bread and drink from this cup.'

It is clear that Jesus intended this remembrance of his death to be at the heart of Christian worship. Indeed, it is probable that the early Christians met on each first day of the week 'to break bread' and to give thanks for the death of Jesus.

It is hard to be ungrateful, cold and unresponsive in worship when we remember that Jesus died that we might live. As Isaac Watts wrote:

> 'Were the whole realm of nature mine,
> That were an offering far too small.
> Love so amazing, so divine,
> Demands my soul, my life, my all.'

Such a response to God's love and mercy is an important

part of Christian worship. As Paul wrote to Christians at Rome: 'So then, my brothers, *because of God's many mercies to us*, I make this appeal to you: Offer yourselves as a living sacrifice to God, dedicated to his service and pleasing to him. This is the true worship that you should offer.'

Christian living

Strictly speaking, then, 'Christian worship' should not be confined to worship in church. The Christian is called to give God his worth and due in every part of his life. And the death of Jesus provides much of the motivating power for everyday Christian living.

1. Identified with Jesus' death. Take, for example, the way a Christian finds himself in some sense identified with Jesus' death. 'I have been put to death with Christ on his cross,' wrote Paul to the Christians in Galatia. Or, again, he can write to the Christians at Rome and say, 'We know this: our old being was put to death with Christ on his cross.' Later he concludes, 'The death he (Jesus) died was death to sin, once and for all; and the life he now lives is life to God. In the same way you are to think of yourselves as dead to sin but alive to God in union with Christ Jesus.'

What does it mean to be identified with Jesus' death and resurrection? To 'die to sin' and 'live to God'? A simple and true story may throw some light on its implications for daily Christian living.

A few years ago a notorious American criminal, the wire-tapper Jim Vaus, became a Christian through the preaching of the gospel by Dr Billy Graham. One day a former criminal friend of Vaus offered him 10,000 dollars for information that would settle a case of libel. 'Evidently you haven't heard,' said Vaus. 'Haven't heard what?' the man asked. 'Jim Vaus is dead. The man you are looking for, the man who used to tap wires, make recordings and sell them to the highest bidder, is dead. I'm a new man, because the Bible says, "When anyone is joined to Christ he is a new being: the old is gone, the new has come." '

In this incident Jim Vaus demonstrates that he has grasped two important truths concerning his new relationship with Jesus Christ. He is clear that once united by faith to Jesus ('joined to Christ'), the old, unbelieving Jim Vaus and the life he lived before he became a Christian, has died. He was 'put to death with Christ on his cross'. All the old sins, the guilt, the shame, have been judged in Jesus, the sinless One. So he is right to reckon himself 'dead' to that old life, and its demands.

But in saying this he was not only reckoning himself 'dead to the old life'. He was also 'putting to death' or 'crucifying' the sinful and selfish desires that still existed within him. No doubt he was still tempted sometimes to use his skill as a wire-tapper for personal gain, contrary to the law of the land. But in refusing to yield to the temptation to sin he was, as Paul expressed it, 'putting to death the deeds of the body, through the Holy Spirit'.

Amy Carmichael, a pioneer missionary in India, once said that whenever she felt the 'I' rising hotly within her she saw in it 'an occasion to die'. Such is the secret of consistent Christian living. It is to be able to say with Paul, 'It is no longer I who live, but it is Christ who lives in me.'

So it is the Christian's identification with Jesus in his death, dying to sin and living to God, that is one of the secrets of Christian discipleship. 'If anyone wants to come with me, he must *forget himself*, take up his cross every day, and follow *me*,' said Jesus.

2. Inspired by Jesus' death. There is also a sense in which New Testament Christians were not only *identified* with Jesus' death, but *inspired* by it.

Frequently in the letters of the New Testament we find references to Jesus' death in the context of some practical advice on living the Christian life. Indeed, it was the example of Jesus in his life and death that inspired new attitudes and gave a deeper dimension to old virtues.

Love, for example, took on a deeper meaning in the light of Jesus' death.

Wilhelm Hammelman was a German Christian whose wife and four children were tragically murdered. Their murderer was eventually released after serving his sentence, but it was Hammelman who took him into his own home. Hammelman's explanation was simple and moving: 'My sins crucified Christ,' he said, 'but he forgave me. Should I not forgive this man?'

The early Christians, too, never forgot the forgiving love of Jesus. It was Jesus who prayed for his own executioners, 'Forgive them, Father! They don't know what they are doing.' And it was Jesus who endured all the shame and suffering of crucifixion so that sinners might experience the forgiveness of a holy and loving God.

No wonder Paul wrote to the Christians at Ephesus, 'Be kind and tender-hearted to one another, and forgive one another, *as God has forgiven you in Christ*'!

Furthermore, as forgiven sinners, united by faith in Jesus, the early Christians found that deep racial, social and religious barriers were broken down between one another. So much so, indeed, that Paul could write, 'There is no difference between Jews and Gentiles, between slaves and free men, between men and women: you are all one in union with Christ Jesus.'

There are places in Israel where Jewish and Arab Christians unite together in worship and service. Throughout the world Christians of different races, colour, social and religious background, experience unity together as forgiven sinners in the service of Jesus. For the death of Jesus makes all racial, social and religious apartheid unthinkable for most Christians – even though they may not live up to their ideals in practice.

Paul states the Christian case magnificently in his letter to the Christians at Ephesus: 'But now, in union with Christ Jesus, you who used to be far away have been brought near by the death of Christ. For Christ himself has brought us peace, by making the Jews and Gentiles one people.

With his own body he broke down the wall that separated them and kept them enemies. . . . By his death on the cross, Christ destroyed the hatred; by means of the cross he united both races into one single body and brought them back to God. . . . It is through Christ that all of us, Jews and Gentiles, are able to come in the one Spirit into the presence of the Father.'

This was no theoretical idealism. It actually happened in the early church, as it happens today. Before the cross all Christians are one, and there is no limit to our love and forgiveness of one another, when we remember God's love for us in Jesus the Saviour. Furthermore, God has promised to pour his love into our hearts 'by the Holy Spirit which he has given to us'.

There are few things more tragic than a church that fails to demonstrate this unity and love. But while it must be conceded that this is often the case, it is also true that this love and unity is demonstrated by many Christians throughout the world, inspired by the love of Jesus.

There is no limit to our love and forgiveness of one another, when we remember God's love for us in Jesus.

Humility was another word that was much despised by the pagan world of the first century. But the humility of Jesus in walking 'the path of obedience to death – his death on the cross' caused Christians to understand that Christlike humility is one of the greatest virtues.

Just as Jesus was selfless in laying down his life for others, and was thoughtful of others even when he was dying, so Paul urged Christians, 'Don't do anything from selfish ambition, or from a cheap desire to boast; but be humble towards each other, never thinking you are better than others. And look out for each other's interests, not just for your own.' In this way they could be said to have 'the attitude that Christ Jesus had'.

And what attitude should the Christian take if he suffers for something he has never done? Does he always insist on his rights? Peter says, 'If you endure suffering even when you have done right, God will bless you for it.

It was to this that God called you; because Christ himself suffered for you and left you an example, so that you would follow in his steps. He committed no sin; no one ever heard a lie come from his lips. When he was cursed he did not answer back with a curse; when he suffered he did not threaten, but placed his hopes in God, the righteous Judge.'

Christian meekness is not weakness. There will be times when, like his Master, the Christian will have cause to be angry, yet without sinning. For there is a place for 'righteous indignation' against injustice and hypocrisy and evil, especially when others are suffering unjustly. But there is strength and beauty in Christian humility. There are times to 'turn the other cheek' and to 'go the second mile'. There are times when we should be willing to renounce our rights. The example of Jesus is our inspiration and our guide.

So time and time again in the New Testament the death of Jesus is used as an example and inspiration for practical Christian living. When the apostle Paul urges the Christians at Corinth to give money generously for Christian aid to Jerusalem, he regards the self-giving of Jesus, in his life and death, as sufficient incentive. 'For you know the grace of our Lord Jesus Christ: rich as he was, *he made himself poor for your sake*, in order to make you rich by means of his poverty.' His generosity shames our meanness!

When Paul urges the same Christians at Corinth to live pure lives in the permissive society of their day, he reminds them of the costliness of Jesus' death. 'You do not belong to yourselves but to God; he bought you for a price.' How can we live in sin, when it cost Jesus so much to save us from sin? This is part of Paul's argument here.

But the death of Jesus is not only an incentive for Christian worship and Christian living, it is also a major motivation for Christian service.

Christian service

When Jesus said that he came into the world not to be

served, but to serve and give his life a ransom for many, he set a pattern for every disciple. Like Jesus, Christians served others by caring for the whole man. They healed as well as preached. They went about 'doing good' as well as preaching 'good news'. But proclaiming the good news was an important part of their 'service'. And although the good news is of a risen Lord as well as a crucified Saviour, yet the cross is central to the message.

The story is told of some Jesuit missionaries in China, many years ago, who decided to omit the death of Jesus from their preaching, out of deference to the culture of the Chinese. The result was complete failure. It was only when this part of the Christian message was restored that the Chinese responded to the preaching of the missionaries.

The apostle Paul wrote: 'We proclaim Christ on the cross, a message that is offensive to the Jews and nonsense to the Gentiles; but for those whom God has called, both Jews and Gentiles, this message is Christ, who is the power of God and the wisdom of God.' He added, 'For what seems to be God's foolishness is wiser than men's wisdom, and what seems to be God's weakness is stronger than men's strength.'

But the death of Jesus is not only at the very heart of Christianity, it is also the chief motivation for everyone who would seek to proclaim the good news, and serve others in every way. Paul knew that too when he wrote, 'We are ruled by Christ's love for us, now that we recognize that one man died for all men, which means that all men take part in his death. *He died for all men so that those who live should no longer live for themselves, but only for him who died and was raised to life for their sake.*' And many of those who have been in the forefront of medical care, education, social reform and compassionate service, and have changed the world, have been motivated by that same truth.

C. T. Studd, one of the greatest pioneer missionaries of the last hundred years, who gave up fame and fortune to take the gospel to those who had never heard of Jesus in China and Africa, once said: 'I had known about Jesus

... understood that if he died
... myself. Redemption means
... back", so that if I belonged to him, either I had
to be a thief and keep what wasn't mine, or else I had to
give up everything for God. When I came to see that Jesus
Christ had died for me, it didn't seem hard to give up all for
him. It seemed just common, ordinary honesty.'

When the death of Jesus grips us like that, the world will
sit up and take notice.

Further reading

God's love: 1 John 4: 19.
Remembering Jesus' death: Luke 22: 19, 20; compare 1
Corinthians 11: 26.
True worship: Romans 12: 1.
Identified with Jesus' death: Luke 9: 23; Romans 6: 6–11;
8: 13; Galatians 2: 19, 20, RSV.
Forgiving love: Luke 23: 34; Ephesians 4: 32.
Love that breaks barriers: Galatians 3: 28; Ephesians 2:
13–18.
Jesus' example of humility: Philippians 2: 3–11; 1 Peter 2:
20–23.
Jesus' example of generosity: 2 Corinthians 8: 9.
Belonging to Christ: 1 Corinthians 6: 19, 20; 2 Corinthians
5: 14, 15.
The message of the cross: 1 Corinthians 1: 23–25.